Road Fish

Tales from Fly Fishing's
Coyote Nowhere

Road Fish

Tales from Fly Fishing's Coyote Nowhere

John Holt

The New Atlantian Library

ABSOLUTELY AMAZING eBOOKS

Published by Whiz Bang LLC, 926 Truman Avenue, Key West, Florida 33040, USA.

Road Fish: Tales from Fly Fishing's Coyote Nowhere copyright © 2018 by John Holt. Electronic compilation/paperback edition copyright © 2018 by Whiz Bang LLC. Some of chapters in this book have appeared in truncated form in: *The Flyfish Journal; Big Sky Journal; Fly Rod & Reel;* and *Counterpunch*. Cover photograph by Ginny Holt.

All rights reserved. No part of this book may be reproduced, scanned, or transmitted in any form or by any means, electronic or mechanical, including photocopying, recording, or any information storage and retrieval system, without permission in writing from the publisher. Please do not participate in or encourage piracy of copyrighted materials in violation of the author's rights. Purchase only authorized ebook editions.

This work is based on factual events. While the author has made every effort to provide accurate information at the time of publication, neither the publisher nor the author assumes any responsibility for errors, or for changes that occur after publication. Further, the publisher does not have any control over and does not assume any responsibility for author or third-party websites or their contents. How the ebook displays on a given reader is beyond the publisher's control.

For information contact
Publisher@AbsolutelyAmazingEbooks.com

ISBN-13: 978-1945772924 (The New Atlantian Library)
ISBN-10: 1945772921

Road Fish

Tales from Fly Fishing's
Coyote Nowhere

Road Fish
Chapters

Chapter 1 – Short Time on a Long Road

Chapter 2 – The Rez

Chapter 3 – High Tides and Green Grasses

Chapter 4 – The Harlequin Parade

Chapter 5 – Fly Fishing For Goldeye

Chapter 6 – If It's Not A Snake

Chapter 7 – Brownian Movement

Chapter 8 – Simple Pleasures – Ranch Pond Trout

Chapter 9 – Bears Paw Mountain Obscurities

Chapter 10 – Maria's River

Chapter 11 – They're Only Whitefish, But I Like Them

Chapter 12 – Killing Time

Chapter 13 – Side Channel Anomalies

Chapter 14 – West Boulder Fire Aftermath

Chapter 15 – Fencing The Sky

Chapter 16 – Wildlife – Autumn High Plains Fishing

Chapter 17 – Season of the Witch

Chapter 18 – The Mining Industry Never Sleeps…

Chapter 19 – High Plains Autumn – Blasted on the Yellowstone

Chapter 20 – A Little Traveling Music

Chapter 21 – Montana Stream Access – Trout Rustling Gone Mad

Chapter 22 – Autumn Distillate

Chapter 23 – Wyoming Cutt Slam – Close But No Cigar

Chapter 24 – out to lunch

CHAPTER ONE
SHORT TIME ON A LONG ROAD

IT'S NOW BEEN MORE THAN fifty years that I've been fishing, and roaming and loving Montana and the rest of the northern high plains. Lines on maps don't mean a damn thing to good country or to me. Montana flows into Alberta and British Columbia and Wyoming. The western Dakotas are the same place as Eastern Montana only with different names. Land is connected, not defined by human limitations. I first thought of writing and compiling this book while working a stream that wound through a brushy, tall-grass valley at the base of the Pryor Mountains last summer. Wild rainbows fought for the chance to engulf the Elk Hair caddis I was using. Beautiful healthy, small, colorful fish. Early afternoon was now sunset, the hours passing in an instant. And this made me remember the first trip to Montana in the sixties and the intervening hundreds of thousands (come to think of it. maybe more than a million) of miles I've wandered checking good, bad and indifferent water hanging out in serene isolation all over the place during the past half century. That time also passing in an instant that also times seemed eternal.

Coyote Nowhere was the title of the first book my wife Ginny and I did together years ago. We wandered through north central Wyoming on up through Montana, Canadian Provinces and finally as far north as Great Slave Lake in the Northwest Territories. This was a fabulous time. One we'll always remember like it is all still happening. Actually it is and this book is an example of this joyful continuum. Coyote Nowhere is a term from Jack Kerouac's seminal novel *On The*

Road Fish

Road. This is not just a physical landscape of prairies, rivers, mountains and sage flats; it's a landscape of the mind, the heart, the soul. Moving through this often magical, even surreal country has been and will always be my life. I ain't no city boy.

Many things have changed from when I was 13 and first worked a fork of the Gallatin with a crusty old guy named Yellowstone Jack. The town I lived in for so many years in northwest Montana, a place that seemed like a frontier perched on the edge of the imagined limitless wilderness of the Bob Marshall, Glacier Park and the Whitefish Range is now much larger and busier, but then so are most towns. Gone are the times of fishing mountain streams in the morning then heading over to The Viking Lodge to listen to Norton Buffalo and a tremendous female vocalist, whose name I forget, play music in the informal setting of a Montana summer afternoon. Yes, those days have faded away along with plenty of joyful things, but then again I no longer possess the stamina of youth to play as hard as I did then.

Yes, lots of things change as the years wander by, but that's the way it goes, and in the long run, Montana is a place I'm very fortunate to call home. To borrow from the words of writer Dan Jenkins and the great amateur golfer Bobby Jones, I've become a dogged victim of inexorable fate. I keep doing what I do fully aware that mixed in with the pleasure will be some sadness and disappointment. Now there's a flaming, white-hot revelation. A number of readers including several friends call me a curmudgeon or terms they consider much worse, descriptions I take a perverse pride in. Never give an inch Kesey wrote in *Sometimes a Great Notion*, and I haven't, though I've redefined and relocated my playing fields a good deal.

All these years of fishing for bull trout, browns,

northerns, smallmouth bass, cutthroat, goldeye and channel catfish have never really been about catching large fish or any fish. Fishing is an excuse, a reason, to climb in our 1983 GMC Suburban, head out taking turn after turn onto lesser and lesser roads with a determination to find a place with good, clean, cool water, a few fish and no people. I live for unspoiled, isolated country, preferably shared with Ginny.

More than 45 years ago my step-brother and I moved to Missoula, then built a modest cabin far up Nine Mile Creek west of town and pretended to be college students. Missoula was a hipster town back then with great bands like Mission Mountain Wood and Lost Highway. It was a small mountain community of maybe 15,000. High and free-form. Nine Mile was all but empty save for some recluses such as ourselves and a few ranchers including the Thisteds who ran a spread near the head of the drainage in open and timbered country. This was well before actress Andie McDowell bought the place and held a press conference announcing that she was going to raise chickens and pigs. Missing that news event is one of the great disappointments of my life. My brother and I would spend the day fishing Nine Mile for resident cutthroat and some very large rainbows that ran in the spring. We had a well that pumped out all of one-half-gallon per minute so we drew water into a tank mounted in the back of an old Power Wagon. We got this water from Butler Creek and also nabbed a few trout while doing so. We'd drive into town, have steaks, beers and shots at The Stockman's, play the Circus pinball machine at Eddie's Club, buy a bunch of bottles of Mumm's Champagne (it was cheap back then), drive home and wake to do it all over again the next day. We had no intentions of growing up and getting jobs or being responsible members of society

Road Fish

(My how things have changed). This was long before some pretentious hack writer phonied up a tale about how wolves had miraculously returned to the drainage. They never returned for the simple reason that they'd never left. Unimaginative, venal sophists in any discipline are unfortunately a burden we all must bear.

Back in those days a fly shop called Streamside Anglers sat above the Clark Fork River and was run by Glenn West, a talented angler and fly tyre. He and Harmon Henkin schooled me on entomology and helped me choose my first cane rod. I remember a day when I walked in to find Glenn tying a small butterfly, sipping Jack Daniels and exclaiming to Harmon that the pattern would "surely take that large rainbow by Turah." A few days later it did. In those days (sounding much like a fading old-timer here) I used to drive down below Stevensville, park at the bridge and float the Bitterroot by bouncing and bobbing chest deep in the river. Occasionally I caught some trout, sometimes large ones, but I really had no idea what I was doing. Reading water, reasonably sedate casts, drag-free drifts, all of this was beyond my awareness or ability. I then would walk the few miles back to the car along Highway 93 soaking wet and relaxed.

Since then I've floated the river with Talia in his Avon raft and caught lots of rainbows, cutts and browns. And I've gorged on Canada geese, ducks, ribs and steaks Talia's cooked perfectly on his massive stone grill complete with Elk antlers. He and I and Jones have fished that river plenty, along with the Bighorn, the Missouri below Fort Peck Dam (I highly recommend the motel there to anyone doing a graduate study on alien mold forms) and some desolate ponds far out in the Missouri Breaks. Dedicated road bums who take great pleasure in rolling through harsh country steadily sipping Miller's laced with Evan Williams bourbon. Good times. Good days.

I originally envisioned this story as something of a lament of great times long gone. Places like Rock Creek, The Jefferson, Beaverhead, the Missouri below Toston Dam, The Blackfeet Reservation. Places I now must share with guides, outfitters and other anglers. Fly fishing is an industry these days. More's the pity. And I planned to speak of the wonderful friends I've made from fishing and writing about the experiences. But, hell, I'll write another book about all of this, and indeed have already written a bunch of them, all to rousing critical acclaim and fabulous wealth.

I thought I'd write about the countless times I traveled by myself in a beat-up Toyota pickup and pulled up next to the Musselshell or Milk late at night, dragged on my crusty waxed-cotton poncho, grab a pack of Camel straights and a bottle of whiskey and slept on the ground. If it rained, I'd roll under the truck and invariably crack my head on the differential in the morning. But the fishing was always fine even when I didn't catch much of anything.

Or I'd ramble on about three-week backpack fiascos in the Bob Marshall in the early seventies where each cast on the South Fork of the Flathead turned a westslope cutthroat of 18-20 inches or the months I'd spent in the Missions, one time stumbling on an unnamed lake (no it's not Island) planted in the thirties with goldens that had grown to several pounds.

But all of that is past. Long past and dearly remembered despite the frequent poverty, the hellish mistakes and exploded relationships. Today is what matters.

The playing field has indeed changed. Montana is way past discovered and some of my writing caused

Road Fish

this. Only a fool fails to see the majesty and beauty and freedom of this place. Millions of us visit, thousands move here. Developers buy up prime land, build recreational communities and try to pass laws that would make the current stream access law illegal or reaching a stream from a roadside bridge forbidden. The people come and things change, and sometimes not for the better.

Still, today I travel with Ginny and we go to places few if any others find. We spend lots of time fishing for catfish, bass, goldeye and northerns along with the trout. We get to know ranchers and people who think that living out on the high plains is the best of all worlds. We agree, though we still fish the Yellowstone, Big Spring Creek and the Madison at times. Now instead of crashing on the ground wearing only a waxed cotton coat for warmth, Ginny rigs the back with foam cushions, sleeping bags and pillows. Instead of Slim Jims and a hunk of cheese, we grill gamehens, corn and squash. We have chocolate chip cookies and tea. Such opulence embarrasses me, but beats waking cold, stiff, hungry and alone.

Much of what I first found in Montana is gone or going. Access to many spring creeks, sections of prime rivers or mountain lakes is difficult approaching impossible. There are too damn many of us and we all want all of this for ourselves. I'm the greediest one of the bunch. The times of walking up to a rancher's door and asking permission to fish are vanishing. The days when such favors were repaid with a bottle of Christmas whiskey are rare. But then gone, too, are the times of insane drug use and three bottles of bourbon a day. Things change and even the losses have their plusses.

I've discovered that I prefer the subtle mysteries and challenges of the high plains, of making a dry camp on a dry, sage brush plateau, of locating a small spring-fed pond hiding beneath a stand of Ponderosa two coulees over from that camp. And then discovering that the water is loaded with healthy smallmouth bass. Or rediscovering the childhood joys of using treble hooks and chicken livers to catch catfish at night. Sitting along the bank sipping coffee when suddenly the rod tip bobs and then dives for the river. Diving for that rod, yanking back and fighting a channel cat for 30 minutes while overhead meteors fizzle, cattle bawl in the distance and a pair of otters swim by with a look of "You're amusing."

On and on, older and older, and really nothing's changed. I still have the mind of a child. And on this beautiful day I'm going to head out to a nearby river and cast woolly buggers along a stretch of river with large browns in it. And, who knows, maybe I'll connect with one and that trout will roll, run and even leap and I'll understand once again for the millionth time that things are as good as they've always been, just a little bit changed.

CHAPTER TWO
The Rez

SPRING FISHING ON THE BLACKFEET REZ IS:

The only truth is wind. Cold. Chinook warm. Strong. Blustery. Often from the north. Always.

The fish are big. The fish are small. Not around. Surfing gale-generated waves. Hard to catch. Easy to catch. Schooled up by the hundreds, thousands. Rainbows. Cutts. Hybrid variations. Then gone again. Nowhere to be seen.

The weather always wins. The landscape is staggering. Surreal. Lonesome. It will snow. It will rain. The sun will blast down. Browning is depressing. East Glacier is a tourist ghost town even in July. Freight trains rumble over Marias Pass. Tiny nymphs work as well as large streamers.

After thirty years doing this early-season stuff I've learned that I know next to nothing about the angling, the country or the people that live here. I've always been an outsider despite childish pretensions otherwise, thinking I was a friend while being pimped for PR. That's how it goes. No big deal. The return my way has been fair. Money for stories or book chapters. Wild country. Huge fish. A touch of freedom. Unexplained visuals that spin around bluffs or race along ridges. Blue-light-glows arcing from the tops of buttes. Extraordinary howlings. Unusual footprints. The usual suspects.

I've caught trout over ten pounds a few times on waters called Mission, Duck, Goose, Kipp, Twin. Brook. Cutthroat. Rainbow. Brown. Hybrid. A rogue Bull.

But I don't know anything up this alien way. Alien

Road Fish

to my soft, white mind. Rhythms, techniques, dictions all beyond me.

Summer. Autumn. A bit calmer, vaguely familiar, feeling safer.

Spring means hardball. All the juice turned loose after a dark winter's frozen dormancy. Moving along muddy two-tracks next to Cut Bank Creek. Opening, closing rusting barbed wire gates. Spending a ghostly night in an abandoned radar base barracks eating canned beef stew. Drinking whiskey. Smoking a lot of Camel straights. Listening to my fear creaking through twisted, corroded beams and rotted window frames. Even the pigeons don't spend the night in this place. Coyotes howl near daybreak. Saying "Thank god" to the sunrise and looking right across the border into Alberta before catching a couple of big fish in a nearby creek. Whitetails running at my motion. Crop duster landing his beater biplane just over my head on a red dust road in front of me. Eagles soaring with more grace higher up the sky. Looking for rabbits, mice, voles.

Vicious winds tear down from the Front blowing everything ahead of their course. Russian thistle, clumps of sage brush, license plates, cigarette packs, beer cans, crop land, ball caps, large rips of plastic that used to masquerade as storm windows, all of this sucked along in a swirling wake of confused detritus.

The Blackfeet.

Yeah I know them. Quite well. You bet. Not at all. Never will. How could I?

Browning. Heart Butte. Blackfoot. Government housing. Abject poverty. A sense of humor that mocks me with no hope of entrance. Long-time tribal acquaintances seeing me as a means to an end. In the schools, on the streets, riding in cars – too much booze, too many drugs, just like everywhere, but way different on the Rez – poison taken to a high-level, bad land, nomadic death trip. High-plains wanderers fenced in by the inevitability of modern change. Happens to all of us, but true murder for these people.

The great American pastime crashing head on where the front is obvious. Not running down buffalo and not looking for images in ice water or wandering after scapegoat seasons. Not a hack, movie-actor's wannabe film trip. A lot of green thunderbirds discarded and smashed along dusty roadsides. Dead men gasping with whitewashed education draining from punctured eardrums. People that could not bank on truth. Reservations not honored around chinookville. Sliding along on fusel oil and ancient dreams. Kicked aside by forgotten collisions with rotted pickups. The breeze drinks it all bone dry.

And even with all these imagined memories and images rattling around in my head, I've often come back here in the spring. Ice-out April. Paradise May. Wet June. Mountains running madly. Green grasses waving ocean visions. Wildflowers exploding. Rafts of cloud racing the sky.

Magnificent in its isolation despite its desolation.

And the fish. The times of hundreds of rainbows cruising at my feet. Enormous, dark silhouettes of twenty pounds. Mouths whitely agape in sexual excitement or maybe eating nymphs. Crimsons. Purples, Silvers. Fluorescent. Life lit up like a natural Vegas strip. Trout obsessed with false spawn. An illusion of procreation that can't be met in closed systems. Enormous rainbows that blast off and blow up a five-weight. Or dog a wind-cheating eight down deep until the game is up and the sullen fish is pulled defeated to shore. Only to be released. To pretend to breed some more. Metaphor for nothing.

I haven't been up to the Rez in a few years. I want

Road Fish

to give the place one more shot to see if good memories, high times from my Flathead Valley days remain. Does any of the crazed, somewhat demoralized magic remain or have I hammered through too many years and too many arcane mistakes to see anything up this way?

Is any of the illusion left?

Rolling magically upwards with my foot off the accelerator on a stretch of road my friends and I named "Zero Gravity Hill" years ago. Illusion in country driven by tilted horizon. I marvel at a ridge of cloud that stretches far into Canada and well to the south of Augusta behind me. The wall of moisture spins back on itself as it is torn between the updraft of The Front and a desire to roll on eastward across the high plains towards the Dakotas. I watch all this while keeping an eye on the highway largely empty of traffic today except for a random semi or pickup. I turn left on a lesser paved road, then right on another. Within a few miles I cut left on a dirt road that winds up into the foothills and mountains. A beautiful, familiar and some-times-fished stream sparkles alongside the serpentine, now rutted road as I drift through aspen only beginning to leaf out and through dense stands of old pine that are intense green with a new year's exuberance. The creek is flowing at a perfect level, its flow not yet marred by the riotous gushings of snowmelt and heavy spring rains. Caddis rise off the surface in the warming air. Clumsy, whirring flight unlike the delicate liftings of mayflies or the workmanlike efforts of stoneflies. A few rise forms mark the surface of long deep glides. This is one of the prettiest streams I've ever fished. Eagles, grizzly, elk, deer, moose, badger, marten, mountain chickadees, swallowtail butterflies later, and a few trout, mostly around a foot long, live in this drainage that seems to be little changed over the years. I always catch westslope cutthroat trout here on elk hairs and Royal Wulffs and Humpies with a light four-weight and a slight tippet. Maybe a Hare's ear nymph down below. The biggest was taken a half-dozen years back. Sixteen inches and a leaper. A cutthroat rarity. If the fish only ran to four inches I'd still hold this water, this undeveloped valley and canyon, close. A perfect place or nearly so and that's enough these days.

 I drop down what's left of a rocky track and park out of sight beneath a thick copse of aspen. Pull on hip waders. Assemble a rod with a #16 Grey Wulff at the tip. At the edge of the stream I stand and watch as a bunch of trout rise to caddis that are close to the size of the bug on my line. The trout work steadily in splashing, carefree takes that is this species' trademark. The hell with death. There's food about. Line is stripped off the reel. A quick cast below the fish to measure distance and then a quartering shot above the fish holding lowest in the chain. A nice drift on the inside edge of the current seam and a take. A quick struggle and a ten-inch westslope – bright, black spotted, orange-red slashes below the jaw. Released it shoots for cover below its kind thirty feet away. Another cast. Another trout. Thirteen inches. Maybe. Same coloring. Nice. Working upstream to runs, glides, deep pools. Always fish. As good or better than remembered. In shallow riffles I shift to the nymph and take cutthroat running about fourteen inches that are nosing the small gravels dredging caddis pupae.

 In a few hours I look and see that I'm well above the canyon that marks the entrance into the mountains. Through the narrow view upstream snow-covered peaks glisten as snow begins to melt in the afternoon warmth. The sky is blue shading to silver-white in the hot light. A pair of red-tails works a ridge

Road Fish

on my right. Sharp cries slice the stillness and mix with the talking water. Bending down on my knees, I drop my mouth to the surface and drink the water that tastes of snow, gravel and tannin. The walk back takes a while but seems like nothing. Tossing the gear in the back of the Suburban, I open the cooler, grab a beer, light a cigar and enjoy what's left of the light. I'll find a motel room – TV, lousy pizza, neon, slamming car doors, whiskey, little sleep – in the dark, In Cut Bank. Later.

This day's been good. Tomorrow. Who knows? Maybe a lake or two. Possibly another stream like this one. The Rez has more than one. A couple more days alone. Ideal after a bad trip earlier this month, one riddled with commercialism and too much booze, melancholy. All this will be pleasant, peaceful, but honestly now after a couple of decades of lying to myself, despite the fantastic country and the fish and all of this, the Rez is largely a sad experience. That's my problem, but a real one. Poverty. Hopelessness. Future oil and gas development. Guiding hucksterism. As a late friend used to say "It's all going or gone." Feels that way here. Hopefully I'm wrong. The gut says I'm not. But then...

... out where it's empty, wind talks. Rain is an uncommon friend. There are some strange people blown away by the electric hum of nothing, running small stores, growing weeds in the dust. Real drunk. Linked together by the white light express that ties all of us in a twisted knot. Mountains blast out of nowhere screaming in the sky. Large creatures wander fearless disrupting the current with their curious buzz. Snow and ice sweep down. Cattle freeze. Minds vanish. The beating moves in constant time and is hard to disguise, but the trick to this is to skip off to oblivion and enjoy the view.

John Holt

Yeah it's weird and sad up here, and I'll always feel like a stranger, but the land is beyond believing and the fishing can be great, so in a decade or so when I'm well into my seventies, I'll more than likely wander back here in the spring.

CHAPTER THREE
High Tides and Green Grasses

MARY CHAPIN CARPERNTER IS RIFFING with gentle energy about Halley's Comet as a friend and I roll down a red dusty road that cuts through early-May, thigh-high emerald grass on the Tongue River plateau. Wyoming's substantial Bighorn Mountains and Montana's lesser Pryors hang out silvery purple and snow crested white far to the west under a plain old high plains blue sky. Not a vault of impossibly perfect blue, whatever that is and certainly not cerulean or indigo. Just common blue. A few puffy clouds drift overhead no doubt on contract with the powers that be for this daytime shift. But the main player is the grass flowing along beside us. When we stop here and there to enjoy this spring afternoon the motion of all the green makes us think that we are moving, that the old Suburban is still rolling along. The only proof that we are somewhat motionless is the absence of a salmon-colored dust cloud trailing behind in a diminishing stream.

  Halley's Comet is coming around again through the speakers after an 84-year absence and we negotiate a 120-degree corner that rises gradually all the way. I glance to my right out the passenger window. A bunch of antelope (pronghorns if you must) is keeping pace with the rig, 30-35 mph, white bellies and tan legs invisible in the grass. The animals seem to be floating on the surface of the tall stems like miniature sloops working downwind on the sea. My friend punches replay, he likes Mary Chapin, this celestial tune. The antelope never even glance in our direction but move in synch about 20 feet away. When the road sweeps left, so do they. And when we roll along a casual stretch of

Road Fish

straight flat road, so do they once again. The antelope are along for the ride – theirs and ours. The song lasts a bit over three minutes, the volume is up and they must hear it, because when it ends they ease off away from the Suburban, eventually vanishing beyond a far swale. Here then gone on a rising tide of emeralds.

We stop in the middle of what is now a dirt two-track, work our way to the back of the car, open the doors, lift the cooler lid, grab a couple of cans of beer, open them, take long pulls and enjoy the low-eighties madness of putting another winter behind us. The only sound is the wind pushing through the grass in a steady, rasping rush. So much green that even the air around us seems slightly tinted, glowing with the softest of green hue.

We say nothing about the antelope. No need to. A coyote emerges from the needlegrass (I think that's what this is, but I'm still working on the difference between bull trout and Dolly Vardon not to mention the various species of fir trees) about 100 hundred yards ahead, begins crossing the road, looks at us, barks a couple of brief, laughing notes with a head shake then wanders out of sight in the greenness on the far side. The grass shifts from the previously mentioned emerald to dark green to almost quicksilver as it plays with the wind and the sun. This motion and colorful motion is hypnotic, intoxicating. Thirty minutes pass before we climb back in the old rig and continue towards the drop that winds like a sunning rattlesnake to the Tongue River. There are carp to catch and maybe a rogue rainbow or two, and possibly, just possibly, and I realize that the limits of credulity are being stretched to the limits here, a brown trout. But remember, spring is a time of infinite possibility, even miracles.

~ ~ ~

Mainly for me spring is about the new, bright

green grass with wildflowers adding their gleeful designer accents, and new leaves on the trees, and the pines turning from a black shade of frozen of this color to a green that glows, shimmers with life. Even hardcore lowlifes like the junipers, light up for a month or so. But April and May also bring on some fishing. Nothing like I used to do when psychotically flinging a fly everyday starting in late February passed for a driven good time. Now the fishing comes when it wants to and I catch fewer fish. More often than not they are catfish and carp and smallmouth bass, the fish of my youth. Though trout are entertained, also.

Another spring. Another part of Montana. The day is like the one above with more wind and larger clouds (this bunch must have a better contract). Working up against the relatively warm current, the backside grasses all but blot out the sky and the sandy yellow and grey cutbanks. Hills covered with the muted green of new sage round off the horizon. The grass is over my head. The new green of small willow bushes clings thickly beside the moving water. The yellow-green of cottonwoods rises above me. The neon greens of aquatic grasses swing and wave in the current at my feet and as far ahead as I can see. I cast a large brown Elk Hair caddis between the seams of grass because I see bugs that look like my fly rise off the surface – matching the hatch with technical subtlety.

The smallmouth are eager, unsophisticated or perhaps they're buzzed on the new season like I am. I catch a bunch of the bass in a couple of hours – none of them large, most of them small, ten inches or so. They fight well. They are much stronger than trout inch for inch. A 12-inch bass smacks the Elk Hair, then rips upstream bending the rod abruptly struggling like a two-pound cutthroat. The fish zips into the weeds, twists the line and with a shake of its head, snaps the

Road Fish

tippet. I admire its tactical expertise. I can do this all afternoon and probably will, but for now, I edge over in the knee-deep water and sit on the bank in thick grass that surrounds me like a bower. The stems and wide leafy tops brush back and forth against my shirt, my face. I feel like I'm being caressed before realizing that I've been on the road alone a few days past healthy.

Quartering upstream and across the creek from me is a long spit of exposed sandy soil marked with serpentine strips of blue-green shading darker with black miniature slashes. One of the strips moves and coils. I think rattlesnake. I always think rattlesnake, even the one time I saw a red, white and black milk snake alongside a game trail in the Missouri Breaks. My hands are shaking as I pull a small pair of binoculars from a pocket. Focusing in I see that there are seven or eight snakes enjoying the sun like bathers on a Riviera beach. I expect to hear strange French pop music coming from radios resting beside bottles of tanning potions. Perhaps this is a topless beach, I wonder. Way too far gone. It's back home tomorrow or maybe on to the Milk River. What's the difference at this point in the proceedings. The serpents reveal themselves to be common garter snakes out for a day at the beach. I relax, finish my sandwich and work up the creek through the watery plants swirling around my legs. I see a large smallmouth, maybe 15 inches, crash the surface as it crunches an early-season hopper. I change flies and close in.

~ ~ ~

Springs are all of this spinning within the flashback-memoried crystalline green gems of time. That's the color in the head when this time of year comes to mind. No fancy-named items, just pure green.

John Holt

And what spring would be complete without a lazy drive around and through the Sweet Grass Hills in early May. Along wide dirt and gravel roads, up rocky cuts and over barely discernible lanes, all of these paths slipping through lush fields of grass that smell of water, the wind, the earth, living. Evenings of slight breeze that moves all of it in a gentle hissing so soft it feels like a dream not quite remembered while thousands of rainbows break the surface of a small lake thirty feet below; or lurching past an old gold-mining operation the road suddenly clears the site and opens to an expanse of green that shifts and elongates far into Alberta, the Cypress Hills a mere suggestion off to the northeast, ranch ponds flickering silver, gold and copper in the sunset glow, the air cool as it drifts down from the top of Middle Butte, the grass now holding and twisting with yellows, reds, oranges.

Or maybe afternoons cruising along old highways around Lennep, Lingshire or perhaps Checkerboard and watching the cattle and horses graze on the luxuriant grasses in the lower meadows as ranchers move from irrigation ditch to irrigation ditch directing the flow of precious water from one field to the next in vain attempts to prolong their landed greenness forever. Days of hundreds of miles and shifting light that end too soon and are always remembered. There are lots of these.

Times of rounding a curve cutting through the Judith Mountains a couple of hours before sunset after rocking through a lunatic thunderstorm of purple clouds, white lightning that sizzled, thunderclaps that slammed through the windows, rain so intense the wipers freaked, then hail. Now the sun shows as the weather struts east to raise some trouble over Grassrange way and eventually the Breaks and lonesome Jordan. Rays of light slice through the dregs

Road Fish

of the storm clouds and turn the emerald grass brilliant, into colors I've never seen. And just for the hell of it an intense rainbow arcs from somewhere above down into the forest somewhere at the base of the mountains. The prismatic display radiates, grows hotter as though the whole damn countryside is saying, "Now look at your emerald." And I do. Permutations, exotic and alien shadings of the color drift, mix and fluoresce all over the place creating an image of a land that is both new and beyond ancient.

Man, this is magic for a jaded freak.

CHAPTER FOUR
The Harlequin Parade

Reality is as thin as paper and betrays with all its cracks its imitative character.
   - From *The Street of Crocodiles* by Bruno Schulz

THE CRAZIES HAVE LOST MOST of their snow. June's strong hit of sunshine took care of that. July is already showing itself to be hot blooded. I can see the jagged, barren peaks gradually revealing their blend of gray, light salmon and purple rock as they shed their winter coat. I watch this steady process from the window in my third floor corner room at the Montana Hotel – the most-likely final resting place for a certain type of derelict now become resigned to his lot in life. No fame. No wealth. No National Book award. No big deal.

   I don't need the smudged, warped-glass view looking east-northeast out of this room to tell me that the small streams I like to cast upon for Yellowstone cutthroat are compressing to good levels. I check the stream conditions on the Internet. I'll go fishing today for the first time in weeks, since before full-blown runoff began in late May.

   Looking away from the view, I glance over to the dresser. The three bottles of Beam I brought home last night are lined up staring at me, untouched, with supreme patience. They know that their time will come. No sense in wasting good whiskey last night on a dead drunk. At least I got that much right. A modest pile of well-used twenties and some hard change is scattered about the bases of the bottles. Some cheap

Road Fish

claro wrapper cigars are there too, next to my wallet. All is well.

The Doors' *Soft Parade* is playing on my Bose Wave. In this real/delusional riff I live in an end-of-the-road dive, but my music system is adequate and the small LED TV connected to the establishment's satellite translates sports, inane presidential speeches about nothing of value and *Destination Truth* reruns with clarity and dispatch. The PC is a mid-level brand name job. So is the monitor. I bought all of this stuff online. Never left the room. Hell, I can buy a Sheffield ham, designer drugs, books, music, bourbon, cigars, clothes, Vermont maple syrup, vintage bamboo fly rods and reels, and I don't have to talk to anyone. Just fill out order forms and follow brain-dead prompts and the world comes to me. This boogie electric as Roland Kirk put it decades ago is quite simple in appearance but insidious in design to my cynical way of thinking. I've got a miniature refrigerator, an induction hotplate skillet and a compact microwave. For twenty bucks more a month George, who mans the worn desk in the lobby, will bring my mail and UPS packages up from the ramshackle lobby and leave them at my door. The liquor store will deliver for a modest fee. I'm autonomous – a contemporary reincarnation of Ralph Ellison's seminal character in his novel *Invisible Man*.

I don't socialize unless the one or two conversations per week with an old lawyer friend from the Flathead on a cell phone count. I haven't figured out the camera feature yet on the device, but there's still time. There's always "still" time. The feeble-minded Millennials and their gee whizz electronic gizmos passing for improved quality of lives can take a hike. The cell phone is as far as I'm going with this neurotic gadget nonsense. Other than listening to the voices that wander through my head (I can have a sit-down dinner for eight with just one place setting) when writing, I'm alone. This is fine. I like life this way. I've been saying this, frequently out loud, for a long time, a real long time. Gotten to the point where I damn near believe it. Looking out the window, now shoved wide open, I stare above and beyond the steady stream of pickups – new, old and battered or combinations in-between, current model SUVs that look like high-tech reptiles, Livingston cop cars with their array of psychotic light displays and cacophonous sirens designed with terror in mind, and lots of old Suburbans clattering back and forth on Park Street. Mongrel dogs leaning out windows of most of these barking insanely at nothing. My eyes and mind slip over and past the vehicular mayhem and on out to where the mountains rise. There's much more to the Crazies than a casual glance might indicate. Enormous cliff faces. Deep canyons. Pure alpine lakes filled with large trout. Grizzlies. The same holds true for the immense bench land running out from the mountains' western flanks. Coulees, creeks, cottonwood draws hidden from view hold wildlife of all sorts. I wander mentally into the stream I'm going to fish this afternoon and imagine current seams, undercut, grassy banks and deep sapphire pools, especially those deep pools. The Doors keep playing …

… Can you give me sanctuary, I must find a place to hide
A place for me to hide, Can you find me soft asylum
I can't make it anymore …

… it's a few days past mid-July maybe long years past. A couple of hours ago I was in the Great Northern drinking beer with the late Norton Buffalo talking about how Clinton and Gore were harder on the

Road Fish

environment than Reagan and Watt ever thought of being. We eventually realized the futility of the discussion and turned to something else, whatever else, and the topic didn't matter. Norton loves playing in the Flathead Valley, especially Whitefish. For some reason I always bump into him and we recognize each other like old friends and perhaps we are, maybe have been for longer than either of us can remember. Who knows? He's playing tonight. I'll be there once I'm done on this stream.

The sky is blue. Puffy clouds cruise overhead in basic white. The temperature is around 80 with the breeze mostly light. The air is scented strongly of the chill water, pine trees and flowering plants.

Kingfishers peer from overhanging alder limbs looking for small trout in the calm, shallows. A Pileated woodpecker drums a hollow tree trunk. I can see the blur of its flaming crimson crest through the green of the forest. Bright orange-crimson male tanagers flame among the leaves and needles twenty feet up. Smaller yellow females move randomly from limb to limb lower to the ground preening and chattering, creatures full of good life. Two large elk loaf in a small clearing that is sunlit in the middle of pines, cottonwoods, wild raspberry, and tangles of other growth.

The creek flows slightly above normal, but very clear and cold. The water tastes of tannin and the snowmelt running down from the tops of the Whitefish Range where tons of it are still packed tight into shadowed corners of barren ridges above timberline, a landscape that moves to rhythms far beyond pedestrian adventure traveler terms like "moonscape" and "alien."

Dark green shapes close to thirty inches long hold just above the sand and cobble of a pool ten-feet deep.

They don't move except for slight adjustments with tail and pectoral fins. Bull trout. Small westslope cutthroat break the surface chasing caddis. They are unafraid or unaware of the big fish below them. Much larger cutthroat hold on the edges of logjams and undercut banks sucking in nymphs. I plan to catch these with a weighted #8 pheasant tail nymph.

The way down to the stream involves a 20-mile run north on Hwy 93 out of Whitefish, then a few miles east on a logging road and another mile walking up and over Kelly humps on an abandoned skid trail down to the stream. I've seen grizzlies gorging on forbs here in late spring and early summer. Elk, whitetail and mule deer are common as are skunks, martens, ground squirrels, hawks, bald eagles along with an occasional golden, hummingbirds and much more. Tall stalks of white-flowering bear grass rise up above the burned slash and scarred red-brown earth looking like visitors from an eastern European industrial nation taking in the sun. The forested slopes of the mountains rise a few thousand feet above me.

The water feels like ice when I step in wearing nothing but water sandals and jeans. Soon my feet are numb. They'll eventually adjust and the contrast between the cool water and the warm air will be pleasant. I work about thirty feet of line out and drop the nymph at the head of a run along the far bank. The pattern sinks down within a few feet of drift and seconds later the line stops dead in its liquid tracks. I lift the rod quickly and the set feels like a good fish, one that I can see in a mixture of muted blue, red, orange and silver through the shifting seams of water. The cutthroat runs hard a few times then comes to the surface and my feet. Like all of the westslopes in here it is firm and muscular but still sleek. This one is maybe 18 inches. I twist the hook free, never touching

Road Fish

the fish. The trout rights itself, holds steady for a moment to catch its breath and then streaks off in a splash of crystal and cloud of fine sand.

I work my way upstream through a wide long cascade filled with pocket water taking a dozen fish of around a foot before working a long deep glide running beneath cedar, alder and raspberry. The canopy of leaves and pine boughs covers the water in shadow serrated with flickering slices of light. Thirty yards. Eight trout. All of them 15-17 inches. Each is deeply colored in its native species spectrum and covered in hundreds of small, black spots. Bright orange slashes run beneath their jaws. Paradise on a stream that is difficult to reach and wade but is good fishing for these natives. I walk up to a downed pine tree gone silver gray over the years, lean my old Heddon Princess 51 paired with a timeless Pflueger Medalist 1492 I reel. The light setup handles the bigger fish capably. I sit on a smooth section exposed to the sun and light a "throw-away" Garcia y Vega claro-wrapped corona. The sharp, earthy taste of the smoke and the way it rides up in the air before being drawn gently downstream by the air current generated from the moving water is pleasing. This place is wild, unspoiled even by the aging clear-cut logging sections hidden only a few hundred yards above me. It's difficult to believe that Whitefish with its bars, restaurants, condos and ski slopes is less than a dozen air miles from where I'm sitting.

Peripheral motion catches my eye. A trio of Harlequin ducks paddles easily in a slow eddy above me. The birds' shades of black, white, coupled with orange-red flanks and thin crests stand out from all of the forest shades of green, the colorful streambed and the blue water. The colorful bands on their heads remind me of the slashes on the cutthroat's jaws. The harlequins, each in their turn, look back at me before walking up the surface of a large, stream-worm slab of rock. This motion is at once ungainly yet graceful. Once there, nestled in the sun like me, they fluff and preen their feathers creating soft sprays of rainbow. Eventually they settle down and appear to doze off. Large trout resume feeding on large nymphs just below the surface of the run, dark olive backs with black spots bulge and break the surface. A slim, dark-coated marten pops in and out of the undergrowth alongside the stream looking furtively at me, the ducks and the feeding trout. He soon disappears in the brush downstream. Dragonflies buzz the water or hold a few feet in front of my face, the many-faceted eyes examining me. There are small ponds, remnants of spring floods, tucked away along the stream course. This is where the dragonflies hang out. I finish the cigar and dunk the tip in the water causing some steam and a brief hiss before shoving the sodden stub in my hip pocket. I look once more at the harlequins. They don't move. Their heads are tucked into their feathered sides. Afternoon naps are in progress. I slip off downstream sliding through riffles and along wet rocks as I make my way back to the skid trail. Fish are rising to caddis all along the stream. Cliff swallows dart and twist in an acrobatic feeding frenzy. I could spend the rest of the daylight watching all of this, then walk back up the path I know by heart using starlight and a rising moon to illuminate my way. But it's time to head back to town to change into some dry clothes before heading uptown to listen to Norton and his band doing *Ghetto Hotel* ...

... It seems that they got lost, somewhere along the way
And now they'll lose their minds and fall into decay

~ ~ ~

Road Fish

Leaning back against the headboard I can see the glow of the rising moon behind the mountains. Soon the sharp peak line will shimmer cool silver-white. Already most of the stars are washed from view by the radiance of their ascendant sister. Norton's CD *Lovin' In The Valley of the Moon* finishes up. I do the same with a bottle of Beam. Stepping over to the dresser with the empty I look out the window and back down Park Street. The gravel lot at a rib and chop joint of questionable quality is packed as always with a catholic mix of vehicles that delivered their addled occupants in relative safety. The noise leaking out of the place reaches me as a muffled wave of chaos. I set the bottle on the dresser and twist the cap off another. Two to go. I eject Norton and shove The Doors back in the machine. In the increasing moonlight and the neon glow of the restaurant I notice a photograph I took at a time I no longer remember. A creek rushes through the forest in the picture. In the middle of the frame is a smooth, triangular slab of gray rock. Three ducks are perched close to each other, heads tucked into feathers along their flanks. The black, white and orange shadings common to their species are distinct in a shaft of sunlight. Harlequins.

I take a long drink of the whiskey, pinch the cellophane off a cigar, light it with a stick match and look out at the Crazies ...

... The Soft Parade has now begun,
listen to the engines hum ...

CHAPTER FIVE
Fly fishing For Goldeye –
It's A Matter Of Uninspired Vision

We went strolling down the river that night
Everything seemed just-a kinda nice
Turned around and I said to you
"There's a rhinoceros comin' – straight at you!"

- *I Looked Around You* by Wild Man Fischer

WHEN THE PRIME GOAL is catching channel catfish in the decidedly turbid streams of southeastern Montana, casting a fly for a diminutive species resembling a seriously down-sized cross between a tarpon and a white crappie initially seems anomalous. A small bug floating on the surface of muddy water as opposed to a glob of chicken liver skulking along the bottom of a river has an air, especially if the meat is properly aged, of incongruity. Seeking the elusive and highly prized goldeye is curious sport demanding a modicum of skill, marginal stealth and an easily pleased disposition.

This late May day is defined by a temperature in the eighties with an afternoon breeze and rapidly rising river levels. The snow in the area is long gone, but snowmelt from the Big Horn Mountains one-hundred miles southwest in Wyoming is surging through the wide valley. The current pulses and surges with the wash of water. The main river is churning and roiling coppery brown with foaming crests that disappear into sucking whirlpools along with logs, drowned animals and old lumber from a dilapidated

Road Fish

outbuilding pulled into the fray somewhere upstream. Soon the runoff will push back into the stands of cottonwood. The land above the rushing water is bright green with native grasses and blooming yucca, its curved seed pods waving back and forth like small not-ripe bananas. The cottonwoods are leafed out in shiny emerald. New cattail shoots rocket up to the tops of last year's dry brown stalks often topped with red-winged blackbirds. Ducks, geese, western tanagers, grackles and some holdover Sandhill cranes fill the air with their calls. A beaver that must weigh more than 80 pounds munches on willow stems along the opposite bank. Cumulous clouds cruise far above the bluffs and coulees that define the river's course. An ideal day, but the catfish are not available yet in this tributary of the river. They hold along the muddy bottom until dusk to escape the intense sunlight and the attentions of red-tailed hawks and other predators. The stream resembles a slough in places where it butts up against grassy banks. A sandy two-track winds through a canopy of shimmering green, light flickering gold and silver as it slips through the trees and leads to where I am now.

 An hour of tossing the baited treble hook weighted with a big sinker yields nothing. No abrupt jerking of the rod tip. No slacking then quick tightening of the monofilament. The water appears lifeless. I reel in, pull the now grey-pink waterlogged bait from the hook and toss it in the water, then lean the rod against a tree. Thinking that perhaps casting a fly will kill some time, I rig up a Heddon 8-0 #35 with a Pflueger 1492 reel and tie on a Yellow Humpy. There are no expectations of catching anything – just killing time and playing in the light on a beautiful spring day – casting for the hell of it.

 How many times has this random act of

aimlessness produced remarkable fishing over the years – whitefish of size that fought like bonefish below a dam on the Marias one day in July, aggressive smallmouth bass in a central Montana trout stream where the trout were just not around, mean northerns in a small creek up Alberta way that used to hold large rainbow. Futility-driven boredom often leads to intrigue and success when fly fishing.

    Fifty feet of line lands on the surface, the water is now yellow-brown in the intense light. The tributary bends and twists in a series of oxbows connected by slim stretches of moving water that gains speed as it is compressed between the banks before slowing down and flattening out into murky pools like this one. The Humpy barely moves in the sluggish flow and nothing happens around the pattern. What I expected – killing time with no fish is no big shocker. Collecting slack causes the bug to twitch slightly. Tiny ripples spread out. The water instantly erupts as bunch of silvery heads and snapping jaws annihilate the fly. Dozens of black pupils circled by metallic yellow orbs then silver scales wink in the splash of diffused sunlight. Something pulls determinedly at the end of the line as it races in mad circles below the surface. Metallic flanks turned grey from the cloudy water flash and roil the surface. Other fish surround the hooked one, circling and charging my fish. I'm reminded of a dystopian scene from TV's River Monsters with Jeremy Wade, wide-eyed and apparently slightly mad, yelling, "He's on, He's on. It's a big one," as he derricks a quarter-pound piranha onto a muddy bank somewhere in the Amazon jungle. My fish tires quickly. Maybe a pound of silver scales, fins and big eyes. I release it and cast again. No twitch needed this time. The water boils and another goldeye is on, staying on top and thrashing the surface with its head.

Road Fish

The others in the school rush around like hooligans at UK soccer match. The fish are all pretty much the same size, same shape and same coloring. In the next hour I catch dozens more that vary only in size – three-quarters to a pound. They take a Joe's Hopper, Partridge and Orange soft hackle, Green Drake Wulff and a size 6 Cree Hackle Woolly bugger. I love discriminating fish. This is my speed when it comes to matching the hatch. Can a Clouser minnow be far off? If these were Yellowstone cutthroat trout in some mountain meadow stream the place would be famous and overrun with whack jobs like me casting frantically well into the night.

Ever the curious soul, I later gleaned the following from Montana Department of Fish, Wildlife and Parks website. A reasonable place for many things angling and hunting. "Members of the Mooneye family are moderately sized fishes with deep, flat-sided bodies covered by large silvery scales. They resemble herrings. They have large, reflective eyes with rods only, no cones. This makes them uniquely adapted to see under low light conditions but they cannot detect colors. Large scales. Dorsal fin situated about the same distance posteriorly as the anal fin. Well-developed teeth on jaws, roof of mouth, and tongue. This is a species of the Large Valley and Large Prairie Rivers ecological systems, occasionally getting up into Medium prairie rivers and reservoirs that have direct connections; adapted to turbid water. Prefers calm waters for spawning and incubation. Food habits – Mostly insects; crustaceans, mollusks, and small fish also. Spawns from late March through May. Sex mature at 3-4 yrs. Spawns in schools, eggs semi-buoyant. Spawned first in May in middle Missouri River." The distribution map showed that these fish are over eastern Montana from the Missouri to the

Powder. Many waters where I'd fished for northerns, smallmouth, catfish and even browns held goldeye like the Milk River and the Marias. I'd just never encountered them.

I had no idea goldeye were in here and in such numbers. I'd caught a few on desultory August afternoons on the Yellowstone River miles below Livingston while vainly trying to catch a trout longer than a foot as temperatures hung in the nineties and a hot wind roared down the drainage. This was a new experience and a good deal of fun. Baby tarpon in the extreme in my own back yard. Apparently all over the place.

Around dusk the cats came out and I caught seven between 8-12 pounds, keeping two for fillets. The next morning, another warm bright day, the goldeye were present in large numbers. I switched to a 7-0 four-weight and a 5x leader. This proved more fun with the fish that once again took any dry or soft hackle tossed their way. The Bugger failed to produce for no apparent reason but such are the vagaries of warm water fly fishing. I considered keeping a half dozen to smoke. They looked like that kind of fish, but several more days on the road made keeping the flesh fresh and firm an unlikely outcome.

Later that evening the catfish fillets were lightly dredged in fine cornmeal, fried in peanut oil and served with lemon wedges at a dry camp up on a plateau that provided spectacular, wandering vistas of salmon, ochre, charcoal and silvery grey coulees and bluffs in all directions. Thunderstorms lit the land with intense bursts as they worked their way to the Dakotas. Several pounds of fillets proved ample for Ginny and myself.

With a new awareness of the goldeye in mind, I spend several hours one mid-August afternoon on the

Road Fish

Yellowstone when the large trout had gone underground, working spots that either looked good for the species or where I'd caught a few in the past. I had no luck until I switched to soft hackles, a pattern I use far too little. I've read Sylvester Neme's good books on the practice, but something about the flies seems to put me off for no good reason. Maybe it's the soft hackle's slight construction or the difficulty in tracking the bug's movement through the current, especially in larger waters like the Yellowstone.

Using a 8-6 with a 12-foot leader tapered to 5x (extremely far and fine for me) with #14 Pheasant tail and I cast about 45 feet to the head of a corner where the water rushed over the gravel and deepened into mild chop. As soon as the fly drifts even with me and then starts its downstream swing a something takes with a sharp tug before racing across and further downstream. The fish shows silvery and seems to check itself, holding and shaking its head, while I scramble in the loose stone and sand to catch up. One more run, circling this time and reminiscent of the goldeye of the previous spring and it comes to me. This is indeed a goldeye of more than a pound with rows of small sharp teeth. After release I move back to the corner and repeat the process. Another fish. The same size. And again and again. Based on limited experience they seem to swim in schools of approximately the same age class. I take several more in similar water as I move downriver. I switch to various dries without success, so I return to the soft hackles, this time using a Partridge and Peacock with excellent results. Eventually my friend begins taking browns on streamers tossed bank tight and worked rapidly near the surface, so I abandon my silvery companions and go after the trout.

What I'd learned this year was that goldeye are

eager aggressive fish that provide sport when the initial quarry in question, channel catfish, brown trout, rainbows, are being uncooperative. The action is strong, though relatively short-lived and the goldeye are beautiful in their silvers and whites and striking gold eye. What the hell, they're not five-pound browns or freight train rainbows, and not even considered a game fish by the state of Montana, but they are natives and they are abundant, eager and a lot of fun. The species is definitely worth my continued attentions (and the two I kept this fine, windy, hot day were excellent smoked). The unaccepted, unappreciated and ignored often intrigue me. Goldeye are like this – interesting, amusing creatures.

CHAPTER SIX
IF IT'S NOT A SNAKE,
MAYBE IT'S A LING

THE THING WAS AWFUL-LOOKING, nearly beyond belief, a creature that stretched the imagination of what can be pulled from the Yellowstone River when a well-meaning person uses a spinning rod and weighted treble hook baited with a nightcrawler impaled along its three sharp, barbed points. This time around the all-too-familiar macabre block it was well past sunset on a warm summer's night, the sky filled with stars, Milky Way glowing white overhead, random meteors cruising by aimed no doubt for some hapless cluster of Angus standing moribund on a desolate alkali flat, a slice of moon above the eastern horizon– not unusual at all, nothing taking place that suggested the possibility of the horror that just materialized from the turbid water of this venerable stream.

    I've been sitting on a log enjoying the evening for an hour or so while watching the tip of my rod, hoping to see it bob up and down in the light of the lantern hissing away nearby. The motion would indicate the take of a channel cat. Members of this species are great fighters (pound-for-pound that shame trout) and make for superb eating. I wanted to take one to fillet for a deep-fry breakfast along with biscuits loaded with unsalted butter and strawberry-rhubarb jam, black coffee and orange juice. When the rod tip did jerk hard towards the water with such force that it knocked down the forked stick it was resting on, I grabbed it, set the hook with a solid backwards reach, convinced that my goal of sizzling cat in the morning was now realizable. A long and slightly unfamiliar fight – weak but extended runs, weird thrummings and vibrations – led up to this now cryptic moment in my angling existence.

My initial reaction when the ghastly leviathan showed itself was to take a slug of whiskey from a pint jar, then perhaps another, grab the Smith & Wesson .357 magnum from my nearby daypack, take dead aim at the slimy thing and blast away with jacketed hollow points. Use of the gun would have solved little. A lot of noise and splattered sand and mud, but the thing would have remained unharmed. As my friends can tell you, a good deal of the time I have difficulty hitting the surface of a lake while standing in a boat these days and the situation is growing worse, degenerating into errant mayhem. When I bought the pistol, I also purchased a large cheap pork roast and a medium-sized watermelon. I planned on blasting both of them like I'd seen the Jackal do in the original movie with the melon in some sort of experiment to determine the stopping power of the weapon. I set both of them on stumps near my camp out on the high plains well away from anything civilized. From twenty feet I missed badly six times, pine needles, low branches and pieces of a blue sky torn to shreds. I closed to ten feet and took aim on the quivering hunk of pork, now sparkling in the sunlight beneath its coating of horseflies. I was unprepared for the magnitude of a rare accurate shot. The roast exploded in a wash of mangled meat that flew everywhere and covered me. I shot the watermelon next. It too exploded in a wash of flesh. I was coated in pig meat and bright red fruit pulp and probably resembled an inept ax murderer. Since that time some years ago I've hit nothing of significance.

But for some reason a soupcon of uncommon restraint mixed with a taste of moderation swirled around my febrile little brain. No whiskey. No random gunfire. Mere curiosity was all. How sad to see a once crazed, impulsive lunatic worn down to little more than sedate enthusiasm. The years are proving more than worthy adversaries for me.

I pulled the fish up onto the mud and sand bank, dropped to my haunches and played the intense beam of my neat, high-tech flashlight along the flanks of the wriggling, eel-shaped monster.

Was it a snake? I didn't think so. It seemed to have dorsal, tail and caudal fins and what looked like a long whisker curling darkly from its lower jaw. What the thing reminded me of, or rather triggered memories of, were the swarms of horrid sea lamprey that decimated the game fish populations of the Great Lakes decades ago. I still remember looking at thousands of the black, squirming snake-like things as they thrashed and writhed in traps set in spawning streams along the north shore of the North Channel of Lake Huron in Ontario in the mid-sixties. An awful sight worse than any vision Wes Craven ever brought to film. Clearly this specimen was not a snake or a lamprey. But what was it? My mind knew but seemed to be taking delight in teasing me with the information – now almost visualized, now gone, now back again and so on until I paused to light a cigar. My head cleared and focused on this momentous task and there it was. I had my answer – a *freshwater ling!* All of the drawings, photos and verbal references absorbed from books and magazine stories consumed over the years cascaded before my eyes like a fast-forwarded movie. Yes, this was a ling, but Lord was it ugly, really ugly.

I think that it's extremely important for the angling public to have an opportunity to know more about this remarkable species. Also many people have said that I have become (become?) a curmudgeon,

Road Fish

ranting and raving about the destruction of our fair land, too many people, neocon breeding rituals and the like. A number of these concerned individuals have suggested (among other things) that I lighten up and instill some positive and even humorous information in my work. What the hell? I'll try almost anything once.

So with that firmly in mind I offer the following information gleaned from various websites and *McClane's New Standard Fishing Encyclopedia* upon my return home from this remarkable voyage along the Yellowstone between Forsyth and Intake. This data involved exhaustive research totaling at least seventeen or eighteen minutes of my life, far surpassing anything I ever undertook and actually completed during college.

The original name is Lota, from the old French, la lotte, meaning codfish. Other common names include: American Burbot, Cusk, Dogfish, Eelpout, Freshwater Cod, Freshwater Codfish, Freshwater Crusk, Gudgeon, Lawyer, Ling, Lingcod, Loche, Lush (Alaska), Maria, Methy, Mother Eel, Mud Blower, and Spineless Catfish.

Taxinomically the breakdown is: Kingdom Animalia; Phylum Chordata, animals with a spinal chord; Subphylum Vertebrata, animals with a backbone; Superclass Osteichthyes, bony fishes; Class Actinopterygii, ray-finned and spiny rayed fishes; Subclass Neopterygii; Infraclass Teleostei; Superorder Paracanthopterygii; Order Gadiformes, cod and hake; Family Lotidae, cusk fishes; Genus Lota, burbot and eelpout. The North Country's only freshwater representative of the primarily ocean-dwelling Codfish Family and is referred to as "ugly" in every reference I turned up as in "An ugly, eel-like freshwater cod of deep waters and nightmares."

John Holt

The ling is typically 15-22" long but can approach four feet, a true nightmare when hauled in late at night. The fish normally weigh between 1-3 pounds, but a monster in Minnesota – where else? – weighed over 18 pounds. Another specimen of 26 pounds is claimed to have been landed in the upper Midwest. The Montana limit seems to have settled in at a dozen pounds.

The back and sides of my ling are dark olive or brown with dark mottling; adults may be dark brown or black with a belly colored white, cream, or pale yellow fins similar in color to adjacent body part. slender, elongated, and cylindrical. The skin is smooth and delightfully slimy, with tiny scales, a divided dorsal fin and a rounded tail. The head is wide, flattened with small eyes and a single barbell on the chin. Some of these things can live more than fifteen years. And a Northwoods website described the ling as being "unlike anything else in North Country waters." I won't argue except to politely suggest that a long-dead snake or a length of old, long-submerged garden hose bear some resemblance to the species.

Ling swim or slither in cold fresh waters of North America, from the Arctic Ocean to the northern US; and also continental Eurasia. They like deep, cold waters of lakes and rivers, preferably near the bottom in areas of low light intensity (usually in the deepest water available). They also inhabits areas with aquatic vegetation, rock piles, submerged logs, and other underwater structures; and migrate in late winter and early spring, after spawning, from lakes to tributary rivers.

The ling, not surprisingly, considering its hideous appearance and apparently possessing at least a small shred of pride is a rather reclusive fish, hide about underwater structure during the daytime and foraging

Road Fish

actively at night over the bottom. They are predominantly predators, eating small fish, aquatic insects, and even small rodents. Adults over 20" or so feed almost entirely on other fishes during the summer, when in deeper water, and on invertebrates in the winter. They eat mainly mayfly nymphs and other insects while young, shifting to a diet of fish and crayfish as adults.

Ling are known far and wide for their voracious appetite and indiscriminate eating habits. Stomachs have been found to contain small stones, wood chips, and plastic as well as the more typical fare of crustaceans, fish, lead sinkers, balls from old towing hitches, car keys and insects.

Early Great Lakes fishermen derided them as trash fish. In the middle of the 20th century, the lakes' burbot populations declined under the onslaught of the sea lamprey but are now returning. Despite ugly form, meat is tasty and nutritious. Still regarded as a coarse fish, however, and not widely sought by anglers, though interest in ice fishing for burbot is increasing. They are considered a delicacy in Scandinavia. The liver contains an oil said to rival that of the saltwater cod. And they are harvested commercially on the Great Lakes. The young grow rapidly for their first four years, feeding mostly at night on a variety of invertebrates. They spend most of this time in lake shallows or stream channels hiding along or under obstructions such as tree stumps, limbs, rocks, tractor tires, sunken bits of Oldsmobile Cutlass Supremes and so on.

So much for educational mundanities.

The ling I'd connected with was well over twenty inches and weighed, maybe, a couple of pounds. I was perplexed. What to do next. Kill the thing and then try and muster the courage to clean it? Or cut the line, grab my gear and flee back to camp?

Smoke from the cigar, illuminated faintly by the lantern, rose straight up in the still air. Coyotes barked and jabbered across the river. The slice of moon rose higher in the sky shading from copper-yellow to metallic white. The Yellowstone flowed quietly by smelling of life – the sweetness of willows and tang of alders, the fecundity of algae, other aquatic plants, the moist sand and silt. The ling slithered slowly into the shallow water, tiny wavelets washing over its mottled surface, the creature seeming to deliquesce into the river's sediments. A puff of warm breeze sifted downstream.

I pulled a small knife from my pocket and opened the longest blade then bent down and sliced the line near the ling's mouth. The fish quivered as if it sensed imminent freedom before going still for several seconds, then it shot off in a series of serpentine spasms like a rattlesnake stoned on caffeine.

"Enough" I decided and headed back to camp with my rod, daypack and lantern. Time was needed to ponder what the future holds for me where ling are concerned. A drink or two around the fire tonight, another dozen miles of downstream paddling in my canoe and maybe I'd take another shot at these weird animals.

Then again, maybe I wouldn't.

CHAPTER SEVEN
Brownian Movement

Another important difference between tourist and traveler is that the former accepts his own civilization without question; not so the traveler, who compares it with the others, and rejects those elements he finds not to his liking.
- Paul Bowles

INTREPID READER, KINDLY INDULGE ME with your perusal of these two bits of informational effluvium. Their importance to the following narrative will become evident.

Brownian movement or motion is zigzag, irregular motion exhibited by minute particles of matter when suspended in a fluid. The effect has been observed in all types of colloidal suspensions solid-in-liquid, liquid-in-liquid, gas-in-liquid, solid-in-gas, and liquid-in-gas. It is named for the botanist Robert Brown who observed (1827) the movement of plant spores floating in water. The effect, being independent of all external factors, is ascribed to the thermal motion of the molecules of the fluid.

And this, also.

The Northern Lights are the result from collisions between gaseous particles in the Earth's atmosphere with charged particles released from the sun's atmosphere. Variations in color are due to the type of gas particles that are colliding.

~ ~ ~

The fish sails through the air. I pull back hard on the oars to give my friend more room to work the

Road Fish

brown trout as it crashes and flies down this deep run next to a sheer wall of dusty-yellow rock. When the huge fish took the fly, my friend (sometimes known as Johnny Surf the Space God, aka Johnny Surf. The name's origin is a story of journalistic revisionism not for the faint of heart. The *Cliff Notes* version is that back in the days when my friend was a reporter covering the cops beat for a reactionary southwest daily newspaper. Johnny Surf had some minor legal troubles while on vacation in Oaxaca which was of some embarrassment to his editor who decided in the interests of journalistic purity to send Mr. Surf packing. This turned out to be a wise decision as he now makes his living restoring classic bamboo fly rods, a surprisingly lucrative business) and I had been discussing how much television has done to ruin pro football – complete discontinuity as in kickoff, timeout, three plays, coaches challenge, commercial break and four minutes of an analyst (as in brain dead jock and terminal sports hack) babbling about whether both of the receiver's feet were in bounds as 397 different replay angles loop over and over like the line on my friend's reel is doing right now, then a punt, more beer and truck commercials, a long pass but flag on the play for defensive pass interference and another coach's challenge with a little red flag and "stepping aside" for a brief commercial break while all of this is sorted out and on and on for three or more hours. Fortunately and abruptly this line of inanity ended as though by godsend when this enormous brown smashed a #4 Cree Woolly Bugger. My friend's Australian Shepherd, Rupert, is on the front seat, his large ears flying in the wind, barking instructions to us as Johnny Surf plays the fish or rather as it plays him. The brown is well over two feet long. This was revealed in its first leap as the trout arced above the water and then crashed back through the surface with that distinctive big fish "thwack." The mad trout is well into the old J.W. Young Valdex's backing as it powers its way towards a wicked spate of cascades and mid-stream boulders. He tries to check the brown with no success. More line tears off the reel. I can tell by the pitch of Rupert's barking that things are getting desperate.

"I've got to pull out now or we'll get sucked into Lynda's Trap," I yell. Lynda's Trap, a hundred-yard stretch of standing waves and a vortex-like swirling hole along a stone cliff shoreline, is named for a woman both of us know, someone who had impressed us with her psychotic personality and drunken raging temper. A lunatic neither of us ever wanted to encounter again. We're the only ones that call this piece of water by that name. Being quite stealthy, at least in our own minds, this is one of our little angling secrets.

"Hang on, damnit. I've almost got him," shouts Johnny Surf as the trout reaches for the sky once again taking still more line from his ancient and banged-up reel. "See what I mean."

I don't, but this fish is closer to thirty inches, the biggest brown I've ever seen on the river, so I look ahead and plot a course through the roaring maze of whitewater that is now only a hundred yards away. I can hear the pounding and crashing of the river even above the wind. I can smell the damp richness of water. What the hell. If we die, we die. I can hear it all now over drinks at The Stockman's Bar uptown:

"Hear 'bout the two idiots who drowned in the river near the storage bins today?"

"What happened to them?"

"Guy hooked his fish of a lifetime and the other fool tried to row them through that hole above

Road Fish

Trump's Landing while the first one hung on to the fish," and the speaker takes a long pull from his drink while those gathered around him lean forward expectantly. "Got pretty much most of the way through, then they lost an oar and crashed into a boulder. Smashed the boat all to hell and they all drowned. Found the bodies tangled in a log jam down by Springdale," and the speaker drains his drink and asks for another. He's silent for a while and then adds, "Had a dog with them. Damn shame to lose a good dog that way. Here's to the dog."

My reverie is broken as we ride the crest of the first standing wave, this one about four feet high. The boat rocks and spins with the force of the twisting water, then we are in the air, briefly, before slamming into the side of a rock shaped like a bottle of Gallo wine. Probably skull popper Burgundy. The current is in control. Both oar tips fracture and are torn from my hands. My friend is hanging on to the boat up front with one hand, his beautiful Garrison fly rod clutched in the other. The gem is worth thousands and belongs in a museum, but Johnny Surf said, "The guy built this to fish with and that's what I'm going to do with it." Rupert is not around. Nowhere to be seen. Next a huge whirlpool spinning out of control below the big rock twirls us around at about 45 rpm before shooting us into a series of smaller obstructions. We batter our way through this gauntlet and then we blast over and into a submerged rock that tears a small hole in the bottom. The jolt knocks my friend overboard, my last vision is of man and fly rod going head first into the river, feet high in the air. Then the boat capsizes and I am underwater. The sun is shining brightly. I clearly see the rock through the aquamarine current before I am slammed into it. Then I'm out.

The sun's heat and white light bring me around.

John Holt

The first thing I see is Johnny Surf and Rupert standing in the river near shore. He's holding the brown trout at arm's length. The dog is sniffing the fish's gill plates. I also notice pieces of the teak floating languidly in the calmer water and my friend's fly rod in several mangled pieces, the reel smashed, lying on the cobblestone beach. Rupert looks fine, but blood is streaming down Johnny Surf's legs.

"Hell of a fish, Holt," he said. "Between hauling your sorry ass out of the water and dragging this guy in, we had quite a time. Damn dog herded the thing to shore every time it tried to swim away. At least one of you is worth a damn."

"Right."

"My life is nothing but a twisted demonstration of Brownian movement," Johnny Surf said. "Reality equates to liquid and the molecules of that liquid, most likely cheap tequila, bounces me around and into situations like a pin ball on bad acid. What's next? A grand mal display of Northern Lights at high noon followed by a July blizzard? Whatever comes, I'm no longer ready. I need a drink. Now"

I slowly get to my feet. I ache and hurt all over. There is a fair-sized knot on my forehead, but other than that I'm fine. We've been lucky, especially when considering some of the other mayhem we've been involved in over the years, driving cars down sidewalks, being shot at by crazed murderers on the run from the cops, parking an old Datsun wagon in the middle of an Illinois cornfield to watch the sun come up (corn stalks were too high but the beer and Beam smoothed out the disappointment). Only a gash on my friend's leg and my bump, though we are out a few grand on the custom-made rod and some repairs to the borrowed drift boat. Fortunately the guy who loaned us the craft moved back to Beloit, Wisconsin for

Road Fish

reasons he refused to list, let alone explain. We had time to set things right. Patching the puncture to make the boat sea worthy was no big deal for a couple of longtime Bondo putty artistes and we still had Johnny Surf's old South Bend 57 9-0 rod and an ancient Ocean City 77 reel made sometime in the last millennium and it probably had a fresh Cortland Sylk line. We'd be fine. Just another day on the river.

    I walk over and look at the brown finning in the shallows. I mark it against a rod fragment. That later translates to 27 inches according to the Stanley tape. I then spend several minutes reviving the fish that is still lolling in the slight current near shore. The behemoth finally swims off. An old, scarred male with subdued colors – browns, blacks, reds, aged bronzes and whites. He'll live to wreck another drift boat.

    "Shit," is all Johnny Surf can say. Then he takes off his shirt and starts walking towards the highway that leads to town. Rupert rushes to the river and retrieves a small piece of the boat's wreckage, then catches up with his buddy. I follow both of them.

    "Well, that was a fine fish and it was one hell of a ride," he said. "We survived. Lived to fight another day and such bullshit." Just as we reach the road we see a rusted '63 GMC cattle truck coming our way. We flag down the noisy rig, climb into the cab and are back to town in minutes. The driver looks at us. He is up from his place in the West Texas Hill country where he bird hunts and lives alone most of the year, that is except for June through August when he heads north to spend some time on his small place at the base of some mountains north of town. He's about seventy, lean, tanned and tough. We've met before. Talked a bit about not much of anything. Another good old boy. He knows who I am and succinctly says, "I don't want to hear about it," and returns to puffing on his

Chesterfield and drinking from a can of Pabst.

He asks where we're parked and we say up at Pine Creek and down at the Hwy89 Bridge. He says, "Don't start," turns around and runs us the few miles down I94 and then up 89 and our rig. We say thanks and he says "Owe me a drink when I see you next," and drives off in a cloudy mixture of dusty and oily exhaust. Just another day on the river for a couple of Bozos on the bus.

~ ~ ~

The water bubbles and glides soft and cool along the far bank. It is the last week of September and we've recovered from our boating mishap. The tall grass flickers gold brown in the breeze. Normally it would be shades of dying tan or even gray. It has been a wet year and this is one of the few times Johnny Surf and I have fished this river or any other stream for that matter. The water had been too high to wade and the big fish have been holding out of reach, not actively feeding. When levels did drop to normal the days were so hot that streams warmed and fishing would have stressed the trout. This fact didn't stop most of the guides from floating in packs and working over the wary and exhausted browns, rainbows and Yellowstone cutthroat. $500 a day for a riverine killing spree. The clients, most of them anyway, didn't know better, but the guides did and so did their fly shop masters. Catch-and-release doesn't work as well as its dogmatic proponents claim especially when a hooked trout is already three-quarters shot from stress. But what the hell. Anything for a buck. Screw the fish.

The two of us usually fish together every other week or so beginning in September through the golden crispness of late October and finally the bleak but rewarding frigid gray monotones of early November. The unusual conditions altered our behavior, too.

Road Fish

Normally the flow in this river gets hammered by irrigation draw down, but this season ranchers left the river largely alone. They didn't need the additional water. In fact, the fields were often too wet in some places for them to get their machinery in for the second cutting of hay. So much the better for us now that the river is finally sporting autumn angling colors. Instead of holding down deep and skulking around in dark holes like outlaw thugs, eating the occasional stray sculpin or caddis nymph, large, hungry brown trout are up all over the place, holding close to the banks near the surface waiting for breeze-blown grasshoppers to come their way. So far, this has been banner season for the bulky bugs. The insects may last for a few more weeks if the weather holds.

We've been fishing for less than an hour and we've already landed a half-dozen trout between eighteen and twenty-two inches. We always release these fantastic fish, but the urge to kill a couple is, while somewhat buried by generations of so-called civilized living, instinctive and calls strongly at times. Atavism making a slight appearance. We are launching a ragged pattern of Johnny Surf's own design, a tragic combination of sage grouse feathers, antelope hair, rusty gold Antron dubbing and a sprig of red cut from an old flannel shirt of his. The hopper looks like hell, but it works. As Johnny Surf often said, "Artistic flies catch small, cute fish. Big, ratty bugs take big, ugly browns. Take your pick." We both like big, ugly browns.

My friend is casting an immaculate Payne bamboo rod – eight feet, five-weight built by Ed Payne in 1950 and matched to a battered Dingley 3"Ogden Smith Whitchurch reel. When one of these beautiful aesthetically pleasing wonders is damaged either terminally or just a little, the experience is traumatic.

John Holt

I've seen Johnny Surf go silent for days after one of his cherished bamboo rods is injured while bending gracefully against the force and weight of a large, angry brown, but as he said "They are made to be fished, not hidden away in the basement like a demented in-law." We both have experience with that species. I watch as Johnny Surf easily drops the ungainly fly sixty feet away and about ten feet up from the tail of a long, deep run, just ahead of a large trout. While doing so, he makes a slight reach upstream that imparts a small bend in the line in just the right place to cheat drag from the current, all this while the cast is whistling through the air for brief seconds. Magical. Playing with cane is sensual. The feel is soft, gentle and responsive. Like a good woman Johnny Surf says. Graphite rods are tools and work well, but cane moves fly fishing to another realm.

  I've begun collecting bamboo and sense a new addiction coming on. So far I've acquired a 7-6 Leonard, an Orvis Wes Jordan 8-0 prototype, several Phillipsons, a pair of Grangers, a 7-6 Montague Manitou and probably my favorite, an 8-6, five-weight Tarryall 2510 made for Dave Cooks sporting goods store in Denver decades ago by Fred DeBell rod. Fred made an abundance of rods for Cooks and Garts (another area sporting goods outfit). At one time, Fred's contract with Cook was so bad that the more rods he made the more money he lost. Sounds like the book biz to me. I gleaned the following information while searching The Classic Fly Rod Forum: "From the 1939 Dave Cook's fishing catalog pg 42: 'Tarryall' 8 1/2', 9' or 9 1/2', 4 7/8oz, 5 1/2oz or 6oz, 3/2 agate guide on butt section, browntone bamboo, 4 steel snake guides on each section, cloth bag, 1 tip 'crystal agatine, 1 tip metal top, wrapped in 6 contrasting colors." Oh yeah, priced at only $4.95! Not many, but

Road Fish

a good start. I won't go into the vintage reel acquisition end of things. Too nice a day to be spoiled with such silliness.

Johnny Surf is one of the finest casters I've ever observed – in Montana, in Iceland, Tasmania – anywhere. I've seen photos of him holding enormous fish while leaning against a large downed Douglas Fir. He's standing there in a starkly honest black-and-white photograph with long, dark hair and a face that hasn't seen a razor for several days looking like he is truly living according to one of our more cherished dictums "Think like an outlaw," or in other words "Keep a low profile and try to stay below the radar." We've both found that life is a little bit less difficult if we practice those four words. We both like people and enjoy being around them, but we are also loners at heart preferring our own company for days on end at times. Then we become lonely for the madness of our species and jump back into the fray. Parts of Montana are still open enough and honest enough to let those of us who need and thrive under such a routine have our curious ways.

A brown attacks the hopper within three feet of drift. Johnny Surf sets the hook, plays the fish as it sounds to hold along the bronze-colored cobble. The fish rattles its head in anger and then reaches for the sky in a series of silver-spray leaps. Each time the brown goes to the air, Johnny Surf maintains a firm connection with the fish and backs downstream a step or two. By the time the three-pound trout comes to his feet, both angler and fish are well below the run and the other browns are still feeding. Johnny Surf is modest about all aspects of his life but one. His fishing ability. I admit that on the water he is a master. But hubris seems to lurk in the shadows of my friend's angling personality. As he told me once after a few belts of scotch, "I can take trout where others can't even see a damn fish. That comes from many years of working water, staring at water and being fortunate to fish with the really good ones – Charles Brooks, LaFontaine and some of the old-timers around here who've sadly all moved on to other lives. And I was fortunate to get to know Roderick Haig-Brown a little bit a year or so before he died. He guided me in the direction of the lyricism and rhythm of rivers and nature. I value the time I've spent with those men as much as anything in this life." From what I'd observed a number of times, he wasn't boasting. Johnny Surf has a form of radar that separates fly fishermen into at least two groups – those that are so good it's spooky and those who are merely skillful. Some days I've watched him work a woolly bugger well below the surface, watched him bounce the weighted thing along the bottom and then swiftly raise his rod. Then I'd stare in amazement as a twenty-inch brown would come flying through the water and way up above the river shaking its colorful body in stunned rage at the audacity that any human could have found it hiding beneath a tangle of submerged roots in the dark waters. Johnny Surf plays the fish fairly and quickly, admires the almost spectral gold, bronze, copper, black, white and red that large, wild browns carry with them through life, and then he turns the fish loose, smiling and laughing – a strong, yet muted sound. He'll turn to me, eyes glowing, and say "That's what it's all about Ed, my man," and he'll move a bit upriver and take another fish. How, I'll never know. I can't see him doing anything different from me and I never see what triggers his strike – no subtle shift in line movement, no shadowy flash from below. Nothing. His intuition, no his artistry, is a mystery to me. A joyful fascination. He takes three more trout of the same size or larger

Road Fish

from the run, then walks over and sits beside me on a dead cottonwood that rests along the smooth, rock bank like a large, stately, gray scarecrow. Or something like that.

"Give me one of those dried-out humps of yours," and I shake a Camel up from my pack, bits of tobacco flying off on the wind. He pulls an old lighter from a shirt pocket and lights the thing, inhales deeply, coughs a little and says, "You're the only bastard I know who likes these the way I do. Stale and harsh. Here take a hit of this," and a silver flask appears out of nowhere. It is etched with the likeness of a sea-run brown he'd caught down in Tierra del Fuego after casting endlessly for eternal days in the constant, raging wind. The trout weighed over thirty pounds. He told me the fish ran him two miles downriver towards the sea before finally tiring. When Johnny Surf reached down to tail the fish, the tippet snapped, but the brown was exhausted to the point where it merely rolled over on its side, gills pulsing trying to suck down oxygen in the shallow water. That was years ago in his renegade angler days. Days when he skulked around like his browns, fishing all over the West and the world with an assortment of crazed friends – Iceland, Morocco, Mongolia, Fiji, the hidden mountain rivers along the Yukon-Northwest Territories border around the Arctic Circle and the vast barren ground flows of that territory back when few outsiders knew of their existence, let alone fished them. When it came to fly fishing, he'd seen and done most all of it. He's had it too with the invasion by image-conscious morons who throw money at the local guides like they are indentured servants. Johnny Surf prefers to work subtle, sophisticated water that requires stealth, patience and vision, the stuff that fails to catch the superficial interest of the newcomer pretenders. Small rivers that look like a little bit of nothing to the inexperienced. That's one of the reasons I like the guy. No bullshit. I drink some of his ever-present bourbon in the ninety-degree summer heat. Quite thirst quenching. Yes indeed it is. I hand the flask. He takes a drink and puts it away somewhere. We smoke without talking, observing several browns feeding along a crease in the river above us. The big trout are keyed to the sound of the grasshoppers "splatting" on the water's surface, homing in like wolves and crunching down on the insects. Then they return to their holding spots. Efficient. Businesslike. Predacious. I love brown trout.

"How many times have you admitted you were wrong about anything?" I ask.

"Once or twice?"

"Glad to say that you recognize that personal shortcoming, buddy. You really are becoming a much better person. We're all pleased with your progress."

"Yeah, and the horse you rode in on sport," says Johnny Surf. Sometimes it was tough leaning against the same bar when someone close has a load on. What friends are worth hanging out with when they're three sheets to the wind, damnit? The two of us have been close to blows arguing over whether a .270 or a 30.06 is the best gun for mule deer. Same thing with radial tires. Toyos or Coopers. We almost got into a fistfight one night disagreeing about whether natural or artificial dubbing works best on Hare's ear nymphs. As for the Cubs or Giants, that's dangerous country, best left unvisited

"God, I bless the day I met you, Holt. You define the term 'friendship,'" and Johnny Surf passes me the flask and says, "Kill it. There's more around here some place. "

He reaches for the flask. The thing not only seems

Road Fish

to appear and disappear as if by magic, it is also bottomless. The bourbon is starting to taste pretty good now. I take another drink and feel it slide warmly down into my stomach.

~ ~ ~

All of this trout talk with Johnny Surf got me thinking about a region I've never been to, a yearning with more than slight Hemingway tugs à la *A Different Country* and *A Way You'll Never Be,* two haunting Nick Adams short stories that have ridden along in my head for decades. How much they've influenced my behavior over the years is impossible to assess, since I'm way too close to the internal narrative to be objective. I've been fascinated with the Balkan region of Europe since I was in high school. Wild, fierce, unknown mountain ranges and river valleys home to little-known species of trout and people who've had scant contact with our neurotic modern way of life. I almost made it to Yugoslavia in 1972 to fish for marble trout, but the frontier was locked down due to an outbreak of some obscure variation of the black Plague, at least that's what the border guard said in severe, broken English as he tugged on his thin, black leather gloves. I turned around and headed south to Morocco and the trout of the Atlas Mountains. Recently I came across a website run by the Balkan Trout Restoration Group at www.balkan-trout.com. There is loads of information on rivers and subspecies of trout I never knew existed. Loads of information and lots of sexy Latin names. With all this talk of trout poaching for upscale restaurants and the activity's attendant loutish behavior I wondered if perhaps the introduction of a curiously unique brown trout subspecies that has lived a hardy life in an obscure corner of the world might at least present a partial solution to the problem. With this in mind I offer information gleaned from the Balkan Trout Restoration Group's website.

The softmouth trout is endemic to the Adriatic river system of the western Balkans and was first described from the Rivers Zrmanja, Jadro and Vrljika as *Salar obtusirostris* Subsequently, morphological differences characteristic for different softmouth trout populations gave rise to the description of three additional putative subspecies: *Salmo obtusirostris oxyrhynchus* from the River Neretva, Bosnia and Herzegovina, *Salmo obtusirostris salonitana* from the River Jadro, Croatia, and *Salmo obtusirostris krkensis* from the River Krka, Croatia. Softmouth trout-like salmonids from the River Zeta, Montenegro are also sometimes regarded as a subspecies of *Salmo obtusirostris* as *Salmo obtusirostris zetensis*.

The town of Imotski (Croatia) was first described by Heckel in 1851. This was, as a matter of fact the only relevant information referring to the Vrljika softmouth trout. According to Mrakovčić and Mišetić this population was considered extinct. Inferred from molecular genetic data, the Vrljika softmouth trout seems to be most similar to the subspecies of softmouth trout from the River Neretva although some autapomorphies do exist in the Vrljika population. Vrljika softmouth trout appear to have originated from a vicariance that split a common ancestral population into large and small fragmented populations 135 000 – 270 000 years ago. The Vrljika softmouth trout is the only known softmouth trout population that does not co-exist with brown trout. Morphological data are not yet available to compare Vrljika and Neretva softmouth trout in detail, but the genetic research and overall external appearances indicate that Vrljika softmouth trout should be given the same taxonomic status as the other geographically separated populations and recognized as a fifth entity within the softmouth trout species complex.

Unless you're in the know – and it is to be hoped that those silly souls at the state Dept. of Fish, Wildlife and Parks exercise as much secrecy on this concept as they have in gating some of the best camping areas along some of Montana's best trout streams in recent years – the fish bear a strong resemblance to the mountain whitefish with a chromosome or two of sucker added to the mix. Softmouth trout do sport red and black spots common to browns found in Montana and the fin alignment and structure is similar. They are also secretive, voracious predators and exhibit strong fighting qualities. I think that there is just enough resemblance to the lowly whitefish and the "coarse" sucker to put poachers off in another direction. The idea of game fish that repulse meat fishers and dilettante sport fishers alike has appeal as anyone familiar with some of my more arcane screeds concerning the introduction of Taimen and Lenok to certain state rivers can attest. This is only idle thinking and wishful projection on my part, but some great projects began as a crackpot dream – think Velcro, duct tape, CDs, the Internet, trading Lou Brock for Ernie Broglio …

~ ~ ~

Last night the Northern Lights had gone crazy lighting up Livingston, overriding the town's ambient evening glow, with an instrument dash green fluorescence that cascaded over the high plains and surrounding mountains in waves of intense light – an uncommon display for October. The next day a blue-black wall of weather roared down from Alberta and points north, bringing with it cold, wind and snow that swirled in thick sheets beginning at dawn. I called Jonny Surf to see if he was up for fishing. He said, "Yes," but he was booked on a flight to Calgary to meet an old lady friend he hadn't seen for years. He said he'd call when he got back, maybe sometime next year. I wished him luck and a safe journey and ended the connection. You never knew what to expect from guys like Johnny Surf. Great friends when they're around, but you could never count on them to be there when you needed them. Such is life.

I load up the rig with gear for a day's fishing and head down the interstate to a little spot I liked on the Yellowstone between Reed Point and Columbus.

Brownian movement. Predictable in its capricious behavior.

CHAPTER EIGHT
Simple Pleasures –
Ranch Pond Trout

AS TIME PASSES I FIND MYSELF ENJOYING THE STRAIGHTFORWARD, relatively easy things in life more and more. Or at least the delusion that such an existence is available to me. Trying to clip the end off of my cigar without taking a piece of my index finger, pondering my choice in the presidential election (just determining that there was indeed the merest suggestion of a choice took weeks), or watching The Weather Channel loonies become apoplectic about the latest storm system (Hunter or perhaps Bula) off the west coast of Africa, all of this is great stuff, highly pleasurable and relatively risk free. But sometimes I need more. So rising rapidly to the top of this delightful list is ranch pond fishing. Twenty years ago I thought this was kids' stuff, not worthy of my articulate and very rugged angling attentions. What in the hell was the thrill in catching a bunch of dumb, planted rainbows, even if they're fat seven-pounders? Time changes most attitudes and casting to carefree fish casually cruising for damsel flies and mayflies and orange garlic marshmallows now seems like a perfect way to spend an afternoon, an evening or even a few months.

Perhaps 30 years ago I had the opportunity to fish with a couple of senior gentlemen from the central part of the state and they took me to a pond of a rancher friend of theirs. Mid-October, clear, and as we pulled down a long, narrow dirt road in a battered Jeep Wagoneer, dust billowed in our wake while we bounced and lurched over ruts and rocks at about 50

Road Fish

mph. The high plains rolled off in all directions in their spectacular washed-out, sere, ochre dryness. Bands of antelope grazed warily in small coulees. Red-tailed hawks circled high above the sage- and grass-covered ridges. Jack rabbits bounded for cover. The ever-present wind of this country was strangely absent. The pond was perhaps ten acres, deep and deep blue. Small beds of dying-back, dark green aquatic weeds ringed the shore.

The two guys unloaded a couple of five-gallon white buckets, old Fenwick red fiberglass flyrods (I now own more than 30 of these delightful creations) with Pflueger reels (one of the best ever made). Two six-packs of Pabst and a pint of Kesslers also appeared along with a bag of chocolate, cream-filled donuts (these guys were pros). The outfits were already rigged with large patterns that resembled a cross between a leech and a huge dysfunctional sculpin. The "streamers," for lack of a better word, were launched far out across the water (both men were excellent casters) where the things landed with a resounding "Splat." I figured that any rainbows hanging around here would be long gone following this fusillade, the trout hiding down deep until the barrage was over.

Quite wrong as usual.

A dozen of the biggest trout I'd seen in some time came from all directions and savaged the streamers-come-musky lures. Rods bent severely as a brace of rainbows fought for their very lives, racing, leaping and crashing across the pond. In a minute or two they were brought to shore, hoisted from the water as they dangled from stout leaders, smacked on the head with a short ax handle and dumped in the buckets. Each weighed seven-eight pounds at the least. Two more casts. The same routine.

One of the guys, named Bob looked at me, laughed and said "The wife, she likes fish."

The other, laughing even harder, said, "She's a damn big woman and likes to eat."

They returned to their work and within 45 minutes must have had close to 80 pounds of trout in those buckets. Please remember, the wife "likes to eat," and ranch ponds are rarely bastions of the dogmatic catch-and-release mania. During this onslaught I'd made two casts with a #4 long-shanked woolly bugger and taken a pair of rainbows of five pounds or so. My bugger seemed tiny, out of place, next to what these guys were using. Size 2 or larger hooks. This mayhem went on for a bit longer, all of us chain-smoking Camel straights, then each of the Bobs turned loose a large rainbow.

I was stunned. What weirdness was going on now?

"Always practice a little catch-and-release. Good for what ails you and shit like that," the other guy, also named Bob said.

I was wrong again.

"Damn straight," boomed a voice toned by years of whiskey and cigarettes. I turned around and the tall, sun-wind-burned elderly gent turned out to be the rancher who owned the pond. He examined the buckets and suggested we take some more. "Damn cannibal rainbows, eat every f**kin' thing in sight. Can't plant any new blood, like them Kamloopers, in here 'til they're gone. Poison the bastards out. I think that's the damn answer."

We fished some more and then retired from our gentle pursuits. All of this took perhaps an hour. Most of the Pabst was gone, the empties lying in a ragged pile next to the buckets full of fish. The whiskey WAS gone. Time to go.

I still have the image of those white buckets being carried back to the rusted, hammered maroon and faux wood-paneled Wagoneer. All those trout, their

Road Fish

huge tails and heads draped over the sides, some of the fish still twitching in the purple-orange glow of a true Montana sunset. We thanked the rancher, who lit up at the idea of joining us at a local bar for a few blasts of bar whiskey and schooners of tap Grain Belt beer. He even offered to buy the Beer Nuts and Slim Jim's for our dinner. We were living as only true derelict fishermen know how.

Three good guys and that afternoon-early evening-turned-late evening remains one of the finest, and most blood-drenched angling days of my life. Classic western madness.

Ah, ranch ponds, the stuff of delicate tippets, tiny flies and excessive conservation.

Never in my atavistic wanderings.

Then about 25 years ago I was fishing with a friend. We were out on a lonely, windswept pond on the eastern edge of the Blackfeet Reservation. The water wasn't much to look at. Relatively shallow, grass, reeds and brush dead brown in early April, a rancher's faded-blue pickup stuck in the mud nearby, telephone wires wailing in the wind. But on his third cast, my friend connected with the biggest rainbow-cutthroat hybrid I'd ever seen. The fish severely arced the eight-weight rod as it powered back and forth in the knee-deep water, last year's dead weeds piling up on the leader. Eventually Rich brought the exhausted fish to him where he held it with both hands just beneath the water's surface.

"Is this a good one, John?" he asked. "Seems pretty big."

"Yeah, it's a good one," I said thinking all the while, damn big fish.

We took pictures and then let it go. The trout swam off into the relative depths of the pond, leaving a huge wake as it disappeared.

A fine way to begin three days of fishing, except in those ensuing, wind-blown hours we caught only three more trout. Three. Rainbows of two to four pounds. Nice, but something of a letdown after the riotous beginning.

That's ranch pond fishing, too. A small piece of water can be packed with trout, big fat ones, but for whatever reasons – the weather, the time of day, their own capricious moods – they can play invisible, making a pond appear lifeless from an angling point of view.

And the best of times at a ranch pond don't always mean big fish.

Early this October Ginny and I drove 336 miles north to a beautiful pond we know near the Canadian border. We've taken rainbows to six pounds here, sometimes 60-70 trout in varying sizes in an afternoon.

When we started out from Livingston the morning was already warm, quite sunny. By the time we passed Great Falls at great speed on the Interstate a thick dark band of clouds was sweeping down on us from up Alberta way. The air was turning cool, no cold and soon flakes of hard, dry snow were blowing sideways from northwest to southeast across the land. If timing is everything, we have it. Want a nice day to turn cold and rough, call us. This particular feat of magic is our specialty.

As I closed the last rusted, barbed-wire gate that led to the pond the icy wind kicked up another notch. This was a gale now with temperatures falling fast past freezing and heading with vehemence towards the teens. There were whitecaps on the little body of water. Thick piles of stiffening foam were piling up on the rocks. I could barely hear myself as I yelled to Ginny, "We've come this far. Have to give it a shot then we'll

Road Fish

head back to town for a warm room and a good dinner."

"She yelled something of her own, most likely along the lines of "Any day's a good day to fish."

I rigged up with nearly frozen fingers, tying on a damsel fly imitation called a Bigg's Special. Works in summer, maybe it will play now. We trudged down to the water leaning at steep angles into the wind. My first cast blew back in my face. I worked along the shore and cast with the cold breeze. The fly landed seventy feet away, sank and then was yanked by a fish. I played it briefly and brought the rainbow to me. Twelve inches, filled with silvers, greens, crimsons and indigos. Fat, healthy, gorgeous.

Ginny took photos and as I released it, the wind died. I mean died. The gale wasn't there anymore. Not a flicker of breeze. The clouds lifted a thousand feet. Sharp shafts of golden sunlight ripped through creases in the cover lighting up the land, turning on summer's last hints of green. The place looked like the Scottish Highlands. Muted emeralds, silvers, soft blues. And the surface of the pond was now dimpled with rise forms of hundreds of feeding fish. Rainbows from eight inches to a few pounds were sipping small mayflies, calibaetis no doubt. A few eager trout leaped free of the water in their enthusiasm, dropping back in quicksilver splashes. The temperature climbed up into the fifties and the vast rangeland glowed peacefully. This lasted for three hours and we caught and photographed dozens of fish. Our hands and feet were numb from the water, but who cared? We'd received a reprieve.

"We caught a break Ginny, let's head back now,"

She agreed, and as we put away our gear the clouds lowered, the cold wind kicked up and the snow began flying its sideways dance once more. We hustled our chilled act back to town as the countryside disappeared beneath swirling clouds and sheets of snow. We got that warm room and had that good meal and thought that the day had been as fine as we could remember.

That, too, is ranch pond fishing.

Insane gluttony. A huge fish. Lots of smaller ones as winter bears down on Montana.

All of it.

CHAPTER NINE
Bears Paw Mountains Obscurities

EVERY YEAR OR SO I find myself back out here mired in this god-forsaken heat plodding beneath a sun so bright it has lost its circular identity and now holds white hot sway over the entire blasted out sky. One-hundred degrees is a mirage shimmering within a realm of relative coolness. One-twenty-five seems about right and thankfully the sun is past its zenith. The heat of the day will eventually fade. Provided I don't do the same I'll make it back to camp and the nearby refreshing cold-water spigots of a rarely used research station with its thick green grass, carpets of Ponderosa needles, outhouse full of mouse droppings and chewed remains of years old newspapers, trailers up on blocks and mostly boarded up, and weathered picnic table. My camp is only 100 yards from all of this luxury perched on a small promontory overlooking a pond surrounded with a dense shoreline of cattails. Vast fields of native grasses and sage surge casually towards the south.

The Bears Paw Mountains rise to the north. I've been captivated by these deeply eroded remnants of long-ago volcanic accumulations ever since I first drove around them on dusty, rough roads decades ago. These dry flats that I'm moving along now are sitting on top of shonkonite lavas that hardened about the time the range above me formed. The terrain is flecked with spring-fed ponds, anomalous items in this place of dryness and sparse growth, explosions of deep green grasses and reeds and more cattails encircling aquamarine moisture that often holds fish – largemouths, maybe sunfish and perch or a rogue

Road Fish

northern pike. Around sunrise and sunset mule deer, coyotes, raccoon, sage grouse, once a black bear, and tracks of a mountain cat in the soft shoreline sands, have shown themselves as all of the animals come out from shadowed hidings to drink before and after the furnace blast of daytime.

The mountains stretch from west to east in a long string of rounded summits connected by easy saddles of pine, mostly the Ponderosa. The tops of these ancient volcanic structures remind me of a group of mildly crazed men gathered in some enormous free-form backyard for beers, shots of whiskey and White Owl cigars. In this heat I am sure that I can hear them murmur comments shaded with soft chuckles as they watch me push through the alkali flats, my boots kicking up puffs of grey-white dust or skirting gardens of desiccated prickly pear. Levelheaded clumps of juniper hold tight to ledges of yellow rock, the plants' fragrance like a never-made gin hangs in the stillness. A chance glance above and I see a pair of turkey vultures circling silently almost out of sight, waiting for a free meal that I may well provide. Baldy Mountain, Pegmatite Peak and the rest of them are looking down, laughing with crinkled eyes formed from ragged ledges of garnet, sphene, eudialyte and other rare minerals. Perhaps this is an inside joke that I bring back to life with each visit here. Who can fathom the humor of the old ones? Not me, but I hear their voices drifting down the slopes against the rush of heated air, at once soft and powerful.

"Every year that damn fool comes here and, wouldn't you know it, he's always out stomping around when not even a snake or a scorpion is moving," says one of the guys.

"Mad dogs and Englishmen," says another with a bit of a feigned accent.

John Holt

All of the mountainous boys have a good laugh at my expense while working on beers so cold they manage to pull what little moisture there is in this sun burnt air on to the metallic surfaces in a sensuous film of condensation.

What the hell. When your 50 million years old like they are and I feel at this moment, you can do whatever you please. I know I'm heat-stroke nuts, but I've been here before and the pull to camp and icy liquids is doable. Trust me. I'm from the government and have your best interests at heart.

"You're wandering a bit there my boy," says Baldy and I check myself, manage to regain some semblance of composure and decorum. Appearances must be maintained, especially before this crowd. Still I say out loud, "Let them laugh. Mad dogs and Englishmen my ass." But I must admit that holding one of their chilled, moist cans in my hand sounds real good. One for each claw would be ecstasy.

I settle for surreptitiously viewing a rattlesnake passed out on a slab of sandstone. Four feet and not coiled in strike, but rather stretched out languidly, body lined in gentle curves, a series of barely discernible S's, the creature stoned from the sun. Its rattle hangs over the edge of the flat rock. Only the thinnest of quivers course through the reptile's muscles. They look like microscopic waves barely disturbing the buff, tan and off-white scales. The one-inch rattle pays no attention to this slight activity.

The only rancher from around these parts that I ever heard speak, and this was ten years or more back in time, told me from the shelter of his truck cab to be on the lookout for rattlers, especially "the old bastards that grow feathers and have hair on their blessed chins." I nodded and said "Thanks," while the man worked on a half-pint of something I clearly was not

Road Fish

familiar with. Feathers? Hair? The mountains were laughing at me again. Was the guy real? Was any of this? Was I?

Crazy business once more with all-to-familiar feeling in the Bears Paws.

What draws me to country like this? There are no sparkling rivers filled with trout. A few trickles that may hold some brookies with names like Cow, Bullwhacker and Suction. No deep blue lakes filled with more trout. A few ranch pond diversion items with stocked rainbows. That is the extent of the salmonid intrusion. The Bears Paw are not spectacular like the Beartooth Mountains with their well-above timberline snow and ice crowned peaks and heart-stopping canyon views like in the Rosebud and Stillwater drainages. Campsites are where I find them and what I make of them. The only people I encounter way out here are the odd (minor pun) rancher driving by to check me out with a quick glance at my 49 plate from Livingston. No smiles. Only rueful shakes of heads sulking beneath sweat-stained Stetsons or gimme ball caps before they turn their pickups around in the dusty orange-tan dust and motor back to the homesteads, sounds of AM country fading on the breeze. Dwight Yokum. Ferlon Husky. Conway Twitty and his *Deck of Cards*.

All of this apparent nothing is what I live for. Death Valley. The Grand Erg Occidental south of anything remotely habitable in Algeria. The limitless lonesomeness of the Thunder Basin Grasslands in Northeastern Wyoming. The isolation is restorative. I come to this Bears Paw landscape to get away from all of it – insurance premiums, traffic, television, grocery stores, sirens – all of it. Setting up a dry camp on a wind-blasted ridge is basic – only the smallest of fires in my Little Smokey grill, tarp, pad and bag for bed, cooler and Coleman stove forming a kitchen and if the need for luxury overcomes me, a canvas folding chair. Hell, I'm home. Some food. A cold drink. A cigar or two, usually my wife Ginny along for the ride. Nothing more is needed or desired.

I've spent a good deal of time exploring the ponds and impoundments in the region. One spring-fed oasis has proved to be packed with large largemouth bass that gorge on frogs, damsel and dragonflies, mayflies grasshoppers that have filed erratic flight plans and even mice that occasionally stray too close to shore. One bass of maybe three pounds, attracted by the minute scrabblings of a rodent, waiting like motionless death right next to the bank, its back partially exposed above water. The mouse moved here and there, randomly searching for seeds, tiny flies, frog eggs. Then in what appeared to be an unconscious death wish, the little grey mouse moved to the water and washed its paws like a raccoon. As it bent over a final time the fish pounced in a ferocious splash and crunch then plowed down into the weeds with the hapless and doomed animal writhing in its jaws. I stopped fishing. The killing, while natural, was unsettling to one so gentle as myself.

Other ponds have proved lifeless. Still others are filled with stunted bass of two- to four-inches. Thousands of them that attack any streamer on the water as though their savior had arrived and was proffering deliverance from the liquid ghetto conditions. And I've caught rainbow-colored pumpkinseeds along with white and black crappie in a few larger ponds out on the flats but closer to the mountains. These species provide great sport as they slice their thin bodies this way and that through the water while battling a light fly rod. The fish including the bass are all members of the sunfish family, and

Road Fish

their flesh tastes excellent when fried in a little peanut oil and served with lemon wedges, salt and pepper. Simple excellences.

The few ranch ponds with rainbows have proven to be a disappointment. Lots of bothersome flies that worry the eyes, ears and nose relentlessly, foul smelling mud, cow pies and only few fish resulting from hundreds of wind-blown casts. One plus is the surreal scenery. Dry, high plains. The Little Rockies holding like a purple mirage over east of Hays. The Missouri Breaks perhaps twenty miles south. Towers and downsized buttes rising like still-life ghosts on the edges of stands of Ponderosa. A sky full of drifting high clouds reminiscent of the Arctic. The streams are okay with sometimes a brook trout to 14 inches, but the best, deepest runs and holes are on private land and I'm not into a turf war over trout. Maybe someday.

In other words, the fishing is amusing to an extent, but not a destination attraction unless you're from someplace like Phoenix.

What does draw my persistent attention is the fact that this apparently dead, dried out land is filled with mystery and life. Animals are everywhere once the sun nears the horizon. Deer come close to camp. One time I watched as a mother opossum scurried (I'm being generous here) past with six young clinging to her back, her tail looping back towards her head – short-lived marsupials marauding in the Montana badlands. The scent of not-so-distant skunk arrives on cooling air. Black bear scat is common around the lakes and pines. Claw marks scar the outhouse. Nighthawks boom and whiz above me gorging on bugs ranging from mayflies to dragonflies to mosquitoes. Bats arc and slide through the gathering dark searching for the same insects. American bullfrogs croak. Western Toads peep like anemic chickens in the rushes below me. Fish break the surface chasing minnows. I hear all of this as stars appear and glide down around me on the 360-degree horizon. Meteors fizzle. Military jets and surveillance satellites pass overhead soundlessly like they don't exist in my world. The fire, small as it is, crackles and sprinkles orange and yellow light in a perfect circle around camp.

The tops of the mountains glow with faintest of silver starlight. Old volcanoes gone to sleep.

Could do this forever. Space far into the universe. Glide into the Bears Paws. Blend with the dancing flames.

Modest perfection.

CHAPTER TEN
Maria's River

AFTER TOO MANY YEARS venerating too many bad habits, the simple process of knowing where I am during any given moment of linear time is often an intriguing mystery. Right now crystal clear water, only slightly cool, drifts over gold and copper rocks and pebbles. A warm breeze puffs along between tall, bone-dry grey and ochre cliffs and bluffs. The moving air rustling the intense green leaves of tall trees, bushes and grasses. I mean this could be a wide bend in the Rio Grande or even a saltwater flat along some backcountry island in the Gulf. But I'm pretty sure it isn't. The Montana State Highway map, the one with the cute picture of our current governor on the back fold, shows this to be the Marias River about a mile below the Tiber Dam that is holding back huge Lake Elwell. Again, this setting reminds me of Mexico but the map says the towns of Lothair and Chester along U.S. 2 and the Hi-Line are only a few air miles north. A line a bit farther up the map, about two inches, says Canada. Even in my addled state the surety that Mexico is way down south someplace and not here rises to the surface much like the fish that are casually working ahead of me in a thin run of nearly invisible water.

Adding to the confusion is this sight fishing for these 2-3 pound silvery fish are schooled up and working the shallow riffles and slightly deeper dips in the gravels. Hundreds of them. Could this be a bonefish flat someplace off of Belize? Looks similar. They race to take my fly, an adroitly tied Elk Hair caddis.

Road Fish

I launch another frozen rope effort into the wind. The fly skips sideways on the surface and then two of the bright, shining fish race towards the bug from equidistant locations. They collide head-on with soft thump, then dizzily retreat while a third one nabs the drenched pattern. I set the hook, the fish thrashes the surface in a silver dazzle highlighted by hard sunlight, then runs downstream, creates some more wet racket before turning on its side. I retrieve line as I slosh down to it, bend over and admire its 19 inches of length and couple of pounds of silvery, scaled flanks before turning the fish loose with a quick twist of the hook. A Rocky Mountain whitefish. Gorgeous as it flashes away across the river that shimmers the blue of the sky. A native unlike the revered and respected interloping browns, rainbows and brook trout. Whitefish. Scorned by most artful anglers as the species wanders most of the state's rivers in numbers that exceed the so-called classy salmonid species by seven, even eight, to one.

I like whitefish. Their eagerness to take a fly. The fact that they're natives like grayling, red bands, westslope and Yellowstone cutthroat, and bull trout. Their lack of popularity with the fly fishing snobs, and the way they taste after being smoked over cherry or hickory, cooled and served with pepper and lemon. Good fish every one of them.

In a couple of hours I catch dozens of whitefish and every now and then a rainbow that sweeps up from the turquoise depths of a languid pool and out hustles the others for my fly. The rainbows leap across the surface scattering the schools of whitefish in little groups that quickly reform into the basic larger unit. The rainbows are not large, up to 15 inches, silvery with lots of black spots and muted crimson bands along their flanks.

John Holt

The Marias River always grabs my attention as it wanders back and forth, north and south around north central Montana for 125 miles before joining the Missouri River at Vimy Ridge near Loma. Back in June of 1805 The Lewis and Clark Expedition camped at the mouth of the river. Capt. Meriwether Lewis named the river in honor of his cousin Maria Wood. Maria's River. Over time the apostrophe faded into history and became Marias. The Blackfeet referred to the stream as "the River that scolds all others," the reason for this I've yet to discover. In 1806 Lewis, thinking that the river might be the main channel of the Missouri, and hoping that it would prove to be a viable waterway for commerce heading north, left the main party and went upstream as far as Cut Bank before giving up on his notion. In 1831 Fort Pigean, a trading post, was established at the mouth of the Marias by James Kipp for the American Fur Company. Kipp purchased 2,400 beaver pelts from Indians who came to his new fort. A year later the post was abandoned, then razed by the Blackfeet.

Today the Marias has little to do with anything as it twists and turns beneath towering cliffs of sandstone or wanders lazily through immense fields of wheat or even canola. Red-tailed hawks, golden eagles and turkey vultures soar high above easily riding the thermals as they search for prey and carrion. Antelope, mule deer, white tails, fox, and even some beavers meander along the riverine corridor.

In July with the sun cooking everything and the sky burned to a flat silver-white, this is hot country, often well over 100 degrees. Standing by a stretch of the river about 50 miles above Tiber Dam on such a day, a healthy wind blowing, it's hard not to sweat as dusty devil winds spin like maniac tops bouncing among the swales or crashing into enormous

Road Fish

cottonwoods. Looking out into a shallow stretch of the river the blue water is roiled here and there by fat carp rooting around in the mud. I find a five-weight rod in the back of a Suburban already rigged with a Hare's Ear nymph, so I launch casts above the feeding carp, drift the fly along the bottom of the stream and eventually into the mouth of one of the carp. I yank back setting the hook and the fish does nothing but continue turning rocks and silt until something trips in its brain that the current situation is not a good one. The ten-pound fish turns 180 degrees and powers downstream pulling line steadily from the reel. I try and check this run with no result. I try again with more force and the 4x tippet pops. Interesting. Strong fish. My carp fishing Jones is now satisfied for another year or two.

    I look back to the bank and spot a jack rabbit loping swiftly from the shelter of one clump of boulders to another. A rattlesnake lies comatose on a large slab of sandstone. Flies buzz around without any apparent enthusiasm for much of anything. The few mosquitoes that brave the breeze and try and suck my blood do so in a haphazard, listless fashion. I almost feel guilty when I swat them. About a half-mile away at the mouth of a ragged coulee that's clearly seen its share of flash floods a band of antelope feed carelessly on native grasses. The buck rests on a slight slope above his harem surveying his realm with natural indifference. This is peaceful country right now. Empty of humans. No planes or jets tear up the sky overhead. The place is beautiful, serene but also a touch frightening in its lonesome isolation. I like that and I like the way the air shimmers from the heat that radiates from the tan bluffs and cliffs that define the coulee.

~ ~ ~

And good country here at the headwaters of the Marias about 30 minutes south of Cut Bank. Coming in from the south is the Two Medicine River laden with silt accumulated as it drifted through dry, clay-banked valleys and gorges. Flowing in from the northwest is Cut Bank Creek, the water clear and still cool. The two streams connect and flow double banded downstream for hundreds of yards – milky brown on one side, dark and clear on the other. Eventually they mix forming a turbid brown current that is the Marias. The river wanders through miles of fields, coulees, bluffs and cliffs before emptying into Lake Elwell, a massive reservoir covering thousands of acres. Brilliant turquoise water shimmers beneath sere sage hills and sandy rock outcroppings. Billions of gallons of water lying out in the middle of intense aridness. The place looks like Cabo down, once again, Mexico way. Below Tiber Dam the water again runs clear and cool, cold in spring and fall.

In the spring large rainbows spawn in the clean gravels of the Marias, the well-oxygenated water providing perfect habitat for the incubating eggs and emerging fry. Come autumn, big browns move from their deep-water pocket pool downstream holding water. They run up into these gravels and build numerous enormous redds. Irregularly shaped areas that the fish have cleared of all debris and silt with vigorous flappings and shiverings of their tails.

For the big-fish trout hunter these two times of the season are significant. Anyone willing to brave the often wickedly cold, brutal winds that drive glass-like sleet and snow into the skin, anyone willing to cast weighted streamers like marabou muddlers and woolly buggers into the teeth of a sometimes, most times, gale has a legitimate opportunity to connect with a rainbow or brown of several pounds. The fish

Road Fish

are aggressive at these times of breeding and fight like hell. I used to come here for this fishing on a regular basis years ago, but have pretty much given up on chasing trout before and after, and especially during spawning time. The fish have enough troubles trying to reproduce, let alone survive, without my crazed efforts. Biologists have told me that hooking the fish, playing them quickly and carefully releasing them ensures their survival, which is good, the fishing for the three or so miles below the dam is excellent and worthwhile.

But this is the type of fishing that flies best when the individual is in a predator mode, and, like my grouse hunting, for now I've lost the urge. Perhaps I've been shot at a few too many times myself. What the hell, the desire, no the need, to kill might return someday. Maybe tomorrow.

But enough of my idiocy. I'm having far too much fun being a loony and bothering these eager whitefish. No matter where I cast a fly one or maybe six or seven race to the fly and lay waste to it. I try to cast well away from the groups and schools allowing the Elk hair to bob and weave its high way down the river, but the slightest twitch or merest surface disturbance created by drag brings the wild fish running and I experience another riotous take, a sterling display of dancing silver, the energy of the whitefish pulsing up the line, through the rod, along my arm and into me. I know we have many miles of driving to do today, but I can't resist standing in this water, feeling the warm breeze funneling through the river canyon and casting and casting and casting on Maria's River.

CHAPTER ELEVEN
They're Only Mountain Whitefish,
But I like Them

AS THE DOORS SAID DECADES AGO, "People are strange when you're a stranger. Faces look ugly when you're alone."

In a fly fishing world where nymphing for carp is considered high sport, as it should be, actively seeking out Mountain whitefish, except in the winter months, is considered at best déclassé. Mention of trips to favorite whitefish holes generates expressions of incredulity and disgust. As the boys so aptly said "Faces look ugly when you're alone."

Many fly fishers dislike the species to the point of barbarism, some going so far as to pop their leaders leaving the fly embedded in the whitefish's mouth, then flinging the helpless fish far onto the bank, only to later admire a non-native rainbow or brown that fought admirably but no more so than the other creature now slowly dying on an upstream bank.

This loathsome ("despicable" and "abhorrent" work too) behavior so angered me one afternoon on the Yellowstone that I charged with blood pressure in full red-faced regalia towards a carpetbagger guide who I'd watched fling the species onto the bank sometimes bouncing off stately cottonwoods before flopping crazily in the dry leaves of last autumn. My friend Johnny Surf and I had rushed to shore. We returned the whitefish to the river. Sadly, at least half of them turned belly up, dead to their world. As I went for the guide my friend grabbed me by the shirt collar and yanked me away. He told me to go smoke a cigar and calm down, that he'd deal with the clown. Shortly,

Road Fish

I heard him say that if he ever saw this "s~ ~ ~~ ~ ~t" again, he'd turn me loose and that I was crazy more often than not. His clients looked on silently. We ran into them on Park Street the next day. They told us that the guide didn't get a tip and that they would never use him or the fly shop he worked out of again. Good news, but I still wanted to deck the Georgia transient. Never saw him around, though. Deer Lodge Prison narrowly avoided one more time.

It should be remembered that Mountain whitefish are native to the rivers, streams and creeks of Montana and much of the West.

Why the disdain and dislike? Maybe it's because they are not as beautifully marked as the various trout species their attention-getting crimson, vermilion, blaze orange, royal blue, gold, emerald and on and on through the prismatic spectrum. Whitefish are silver that runs to brown nearing black along their backs with some showing shades of bronze. Shadings of royal blue and purple are common. Their mouths and the rest of them for that matter bear some resemblance to suckers, a big-time shortcoming in the fly fishing world unless you're a bonefish.

Is this unpopularity generated because they rarely jump when hooked, though the same can be said of bull trout, and many browns and brook trout; or perhaps their un-trout-like appearance lacking rainbow colors but featuring scales like a sucker (and a bonefish)?

On a hot July morning I was taking good-sized browns on a #14 Yellow Humpy that was approximating the modest hatch of golden stoneflies. The browns were cooperative. The fishing was easy. Enjoyable. Then a mountain whitefish sucked in the Humpy. In the shallow clear water its coloration and shape were recognizable. Not wanting to upset the casually working browns, I stripped the fish to me, but then it began to circle around and I followed its motions spinning like a one-man merry-go-round. One rotation. Two. Three. Wild Man Fischer lives. Then the fish stopped and let me release it. The 14-inch whitefish wandered off downstream. If ever there was a fly fishing metaphor for the absurdity of life, this was it – a one-man traveling carnival spinning clumsily in the middle of a small high plains stream. I walked to the bank laughing at myself. Lit a cigar and watched the browns and whitefish feed on the bugs. No hubris here. Just another minor variation on Firesign Theatre's "How can you be two places at once when you're really nowhere at all?" theme.

Perhaps the two main reasons for their unpopularity among anglers that borders on fly fishing xenophobia are the fact that mountain whitefish out-number trout in most rivers by ratios of six-to-one, even eight-to-one. In rivers such as the Kootenai, Yellowstone, and Flathead the figure is greater still. In the Madison River, mountain whitefish densities reach 15,000 fish per mile. Compare this to 6,000 trout per mile in the Bighorn, a river renowned for its astonishing numbers of large fish. Montana Dept. of Fish Wildlife and Parks fisheries biologist John Fraley said in an article for *Montana Outdoors*, "While conducting underwater fish surveys in the South and Middle forks of the Flathead, I've seen portions of the stream bottom completely covered with mountain whitefish," a nice vindication that what I'm seeing on this river is really happening.

Whitefish don't directly compete with trout for food, habitat or spawning areas on a regular basis or trout would be in big trouble. The following paragraph is from the Montana Fish, Wildlife and Parks website where the agency classifies Mountain whitefish as a gamefish:

"Whitefish feed on aquatic insects on the stream

Road Fish

bottom and usually occupy the lower stretches of a pool. Trout often feed in different locations of the water column of a river ... They are considered a nuisance by some anglers, but are sought after by others. Whitefish provide forage for larger trout. They have evolved with our native trout and have been shown to provide little competition with trout. Their pointed snout and small round mouth makes them efficient at vacuuming invertebrates from the substrate while trout tend to feed more on drifting insects. Mountain whitefish often congregate in large schools on their fall-spawning runs to broadcast their adhesive eggs over gravel bars in tributary streams. Mountain whitefish are one of our most important native gamefish because of their abundance and willingness to take a bait or artificial fly...Competition with trout is probably slight as they use different areas in a body of water. Whitefish feed mostly from the bottom whereas most trout feed of drift out of the water column."

As mentioned above, trout often feed in different locations of the water column of a river when whitefish are eating, though they can make taking trout on dries difficult to nearly impossible at times. Whitefish generally occupy the lower, deeper ends of pools. Due to the abundance of the species, anglers may keep 100 whitefish. In my favorite small streams a whitefish of three pounds is a rarity. They seem to average about half this weight. Their flesh is superb when lightly brined with brown sugar, bay leaves, kosher salt and cracked pepper then smoked over cherry wood (but so is trout, but I'm not in the mood to wander down that land-mined two-track).

Another reason for their low standing among fly fishers is that they are easy to catch. During an evening's rise on the Jefferson one time I had difficulty in not catching whitefish and was taking about eight or nine of them to each brown. The action was beyond steady, but as time passed I grew tired of hauling in (gratuitous Latin usage alert) Prosopium williamsoni and releasing them. Always a champion of this native piscatorial son I was sliding into the noisome country of the hypocrite. The concomitant arrival of wind with settling darkness saved me from this situation. And drifting a nymph, any nymph, any size, even big Buggers, among them causes the fish to quiver with excitement and fight for position as the fly tumbles along, the whitefish bumping and jostling among themselves like boozers waiting for post time outside a bar on Sunday morning – shake, rattle and roll.

 After moving along the bank downstream of the whitefish herd and then wading out to a shallow gravel bar in mid-stream, I cast a Marabou Muddler minnow into the center of the mass of fish for the hell of it. I was using a Heddon 8-6 #14 Thoroughbred, a venerable and utilitarian bamboo rod that is one of my favorites. I realize that I'm courting angling shunning with this type of behavior, but it was a throw-caution-to-the-wind kind of day. Would they hit this streamer or flee for their very lives at the abrupt intrusion of this alien terror in their midst. I watched as the Muddler sank down slowly in the clear water, the current imparting a slight sense of verisimilitude to its motion. The fish seemed oblivious until the pattern dropped top of them, apparently an event in whitefish circles that announced the apocalypse as they fled from the fly leaving a large circle of the streambed free of their kind.

 Eventually they drifted back to the moribund Muddler and gave it a thorough inspection. Finally one of them, a stout one with part of its dorsal fin missing, attacked the pattern with a motion that resembled a

Road Fish

fish's version of a pounce. The ensuing struggle scattered the others. When I set the whitefish free it dashed off to join its mates. In minutes they returned. The one with the damaged fin was with them. Before any others in the herd could grab the Muddler, this guy took the fly again and dashed off downstream.

    I admire that level of enthusiasm and the species in general. One of many reasons I venerate the lowly mountain whitefish. A willingness to keep trying counts for a lot in my life.

CHAPTER TWELVE
Killing Time

THE LAST OF THE LIGHT WAS GOING, drifting away with an orange-gold edge that crept lazily up the cone-shaped butte while silently pulling purple and steel blues behind as the sun dropped away behind the Rocky Mountain Front one-hundred miles to the west. In windy land that always seems to be blowing somewhere, strangely, the air was flat calm and so was the surface of the small lake, no ragged waves whipped white by eighty-mile-an-hour gusts roaring across the prairie and shooting up the draws. Though in this uncommon stillness the water was far from lifeless. Countless rainbows dimpled the surface. Little ones of six inches, medium ones, and here and there large fish of several pounds or more. Sippings, splashings and slurpings – the sounds of fish eating without a worry in the world. They were casually feeding on some small bug of mayfly dimensions, probably some mutant callibaetis sub-species spawned by the incredible isolation and stark raving lonesomeness of this place. The last of the summer's heat was dying a peaceful mid-September death out here above Montana's Hi-Line not far below the Alberta border. The Sweet Grass Hills – West, Middle, East and the slightly lesser entities of Mt. Lebanon and Haystack Butte. Middle towered above us casting a serious reflection on the still water. The evening was turning cool. The trout seemed to take no notice of this or the fading light show. They just kept sipping away making their liquid, crystalline sounds. Soft music swiftly sucked dry by the waves of tan grama and buffalo grass holding motionless. Miles and miles of the stuff languidly fading into autumn.

I launched a cast of about seventy feet out ahead of a rise made by a worthy trout and got lucky when it sucked down the fly, setting the hook in its voracious vehemence. Feeling the bite of the point galvanized the rainbow into a series of leaps towards the far shore, water spraying in sheets. The fish crashed across the lake, putting down everything in its path except for a group of mallards that lifted immediately into the air with beating wings and disturbed "Quacks." They were out of sight over a near ridge in seconds bound for quieter doings in some other puddle.

The fishing went like this until deep dark and I kept a few smaller ones for dinner. I liked the taste of trout sautéed in olive oil and butter with a handful of slivered almonds thrown in. Salt, pepper and a squeeze of lime juice and that was that. Walking up the rise from the lakeshore I looked up and saw the sky filled with stars hanging in three-dimensional relief against the blackness. A crescent moon was showing itself silvery as it rose east of the far away lights of the railroad town of Shelby. Coyotes howled in acknowledgment from the tops of flattened hills. Ginny and I cooked the fish in a pan on a Coleman stove. No fires here. Too dry and no wood to speak of, except for wiry tangles of sage. No trees out in the huge openness.

There really wasn't anything special to this place. Nothing much to it. A trio of volcanic-shaped buttes, three towering cones, standing alone together out here like a miniature mountain range. There are other places we know about, had spent time in like the Missouri Breaks a few hours away. A place where the river flows large and silent. Where elk the size of draft horses rise up out of brushy cuts in the land around sunset. Where thunder and lightning appear from all directions all at once out of nowhere and pound the land with such intensity that praying for survival seems the natural thing to do. We'd had times there where even bouncing and lurching across a bone-dry dirt two-track required four-wheel drive if we were to reach a little-known lake filled with voracious three-inch largemouth bass. And there was the morning in that country when we woke to the sound of a pick-up truck slamming on its brakes near camp. A government biologist was heading out to the field. We were pulling an Avon raft we'd used to float the Missouri below Fort Peck Dam and other lesser flows. The anomalous sight of the craft out here made the woman driver look once. Drive off. Stop. Look again. Repeat the sequence then roar off to a plague-infested prairie dog town. She obviously preferred studying the Black Death to possibly dealing with lunatic fly fishers ensconced in the middle of a desert. Or there are all those lakes along The Front over by Augusta filled with over-weight browns and just as fat rainbows. We've caught plenty of those with the rocky reefs of the mountains holding silently in the background.

So where we were now is no big deal, even if a Canadian mining company eventually has its way and tears the gold out of the butte rising above the lake we just fished. We can go elsewhere and for that matter even come back here and catch these fish while we watch the butte being leveled with tons of explosives, and then see the blasted rock hauled away by a horde of massive earth-moving machines. It is all the same to us. As Annie Dillard said in an article for Harper's "We arise from dirt and dwindle to dirt, and the might of the universe is arrayed against us."

That gets it. No big deal.

After eating the rainbows we stand in the star-bright darkness looking at the shadows we cast when far in the distance we spot headlights climbing and dipping, moving in our direction like a spastic searchlight. A car or truck is heading towards us on the only road in, a dusty job that wanders through wheat fields and rangeland. We watch as the car approaches. It stops every now and then to open and close a barbed-wire gate before moving ahead. Eventually we can hear the faint whine of its engine, the sound drifting unnaturally to us. The air is so clear up here that we can see ranch lights many miles away and the observed car's approach over a period of thirty minutes or so. We wonder if the vehicle is full of sex-crazed, carousing teenagers from nearby Sunburst or even worse, axe murderers looking for random victims like us. We've been random victims all our lives. In fact, we are quite good at it. I long for the .357 magnum I'd left on the kitchen table yesterday. Eventually the car, an old Japanese beater from the sounds of the muffler and the rotten exhaust smell, drives by us and stops nearby at the next gate in the road. We hear the muffled, bass booming of the sound system, not at all like the booming of night owls slicing through the air above us. Then the car backs up and turns around. "God. They're leaving," we think, but are wrong as usual. The car rolls by, pulls down to the water not too far from us, and stops.

    All is quiet, even the car's music. Then the inside light flashes on and stays that way. Then goes off. Then on again. This continues for an hour or so. Ginny walks over to our rig and grabs a pair of binoculars. She creeps to within yards of the car and begins spying on the car's occupants. I slip up behind her and take a look through the glasses. When the inside light goes on I could see a pair of guys, in their twenties, passing something back and forth. A cigarette lighter flickers on and off and clouds of smoke filled the interior. The image is so cloudy it looks like one of my photographs. This activity goes on well into the night. The moon, now a copper crescent, is dropping down towards the southeastern horizon. We finally give up and sneak back to camp reasonably assured that the two smokers of what obviously isn't pipe tobacco, a smell of something much more aromatic, herbal, reaches us on the slight evening breeze, aren't out this way to do us wrong.

"Over 130 years of living between us and look at what we do for amusement," I laugh.

"It's pathetic, John," and we both laugh and then crawl into our cold sleeping bags. If the two in the car are indeed dope fiends, as a rule ruthless individuals every one of them, they are too well-tuned by now to bother us. If we have grievously slighted their character and they are merely axe murders, well, our lifeless, sightless heads will be looking out on wide, open Montana for eternity.

The intense light of a new day's sun flashing over the eastern hills wakes us. It is nippy out and there is frost on the ground, but at least our heads are still attached. Looking down to the lake we notice that the car is gone and so are our un-met friends. Following a breakfast of thick Ethiopian coffee, Krusteez pancakes covered with butter and Vermont maple syrup, and some bananas we head down to the water for a dip. Mid-morning and already eighty degrees. Another blown away gorgeous late-summer day. We strip and jump in the water. Definitely awake now. As we paddle around like confused Springer Spaniels, tiny trout nibble at the hairs on our bodies. I hope that the sun's intensity will keep much larger trout holding tight to the lake's bottom. After a while we climb out and dry off in the warming air. Not a cloud in sight. Nothing. And then small rise forms out in the middle. Little fish. Then more and more. Larger ripples. The wind is still a dead issue but the lake is dancing. Perhaps we'd chase the rainbows later, for now we prefer being voyeurs once again.

CHAPTER THIRTEEN
Side Channel Anomalies

WE LIKE TO FISH SIDE CHANNELS of the larger rivers out here including this 80-mile stretch of the Yellowstone between Livingston and Columbus for a variety of reasons, some of them even approaching sensible. They are secluded and relatively unfished compared to the main river and they cut big water down to size make wading and presentation a simpler and easier proposition. That's why we're here on this late July afternoon casting hopper patterns in the heat beneath a blue sky that last saw clouds a few days ago. We've taken browns, rainbows and several Yellowstone cutthroat to twenty inches. Easy, enjoyable fishing with a curious bonus. According to most anglers and guides (who know everything about the rivers they think belong to only them) there are not supposed to be any cutthroat in this stretch of the river. They belong way back upstream closer to Big Timber according to the experts. Well, we know what cutthroat look like and these are them. What can we say?

As we ready to cross the channel and walk back down a dusty ranch road to our camp a whirling, hissing sound grabs our attention. Looking across the water we see a devil wind that is approaching tornadadic proportions. The dirty brown-grey thing is tearing out junipers, remnants of an abandoned apple orchard and brush before turning its attention to a boulder the size of an old Austin Mini circa 1965, the real ones. The spinning entity envelopes the rock with a loud clatter and more hissing, lifts the thing that must weigh a couple of tons several feet off the ground

Road Fish

before depositing it in a deep run we were planning to fish with a tremendous splash. Then the devil wind dissipates, disappears into the hot air like it was never there in the first place.

We look at each other and shrug. Never seen that one before. The mini tornado was a bit unsettling, but by the time we're halfway back to camp and a needed lunch, the entire experience feels surreal in a dreamlike way, the type of deal that vanishes into the thin air of memory the more you try and recall the experience. Soon this, like so many aspects of our lives, would be like they never happened at all. Nothing more than delusions.

~ ~ ~

The drive to the stretch of river we planned to fish today and tomorrow along I90 followed the Yellowstone for the entire 75 miles. We didn't see a raft or drift boat the whole time when normally there'd be a dozen or more scattered along the 60 miles of prime trout water. The heat and smoke had driven most fly fishers off the water. Livingston was beginning to resemble a ghost town or at least a modest asylum without walls.

By late morning a summer wind had come up, the temperature near 90. Smoke from forest fires raging out of control west of here in Idaho and Washington washed the sky of its crisp blue and turned things eerily dirty white. This was an annual occurrence. Those of us who call the West home deal with the danger and attendant destruction as best we can. We don't like them but we get through it one way or another each tinder-dry fire season, a time when some creeks go dry, river levels plummet and the ground duff of needles and leaves crackles beneath your boots. When we stop at the campground on the river, the air smells of the smoke from the conflagrations to the west. Looking up river is like seeing the world through a gauze filter – things up close appearing surreal with that strange reality fading away into a wall of smoke after a half mile or less. Our Springer, Bouchee, caroused along the river.

We left the food in the Suburban, rigged our rods and struck off to where we intended to fish, a series of side channels with subtle currents that always held large, fat brown and Yellowstone cutthroat trout. Bouchee picked up on our movement upstream and was soon loping from side to side on the dirt and gravel ranch road, nose tight to the ground. He'd be frolicking in the water when we reached our destination. Aside from the smoke it was a gorgeous high summer day. When we cut down to the bank of the river and pushed through tall green turning to warm brown grass kicking up thousands of grasshoppers, legs clacking as they flew, glided and caromed into each other or were swept out over the water on a gust of wind. The trout were waiting and we watched as they chased down the doomed insects, the fish slashing and devouring their prey like marauding freshwater sharks. Our fly pattern selection had been made for us. We would use large Joe's Hoppers, my favorite imitation of the creatures cavorting all around us. Bouchee was now plowing through the grass snapping at the grasshoppers like the fish in the river. His teeth making clacking sounds as he chomped down on the bugs. He'd have his fill in minutes. This wasn't his first grasshopper rodeo. He was standing chest deep in the slow water by the gravel bank when we caught up with him. Now the sounds of his thirsty slurpings replaced the noise of his insectivorous feeding frenzy only recently completed.

Ginny and I laughed at the dog, the beauty of this day despite the smoke, this wondrous spot and being with each other. This was good. I needed more of this

Road Fish

type of life. I'd become too much the cynic and something of a grouch while writing over the winter. We fished for a couple of hours or so catching cutthroat after fat cutthroat along with a few really big browns on the hopper pattern. Ginny cast nicely, the line streaking behind her in a tight loop then shooting forward 40 feet to land delicately on the spot she's selected while making her back cast, a period of at most one second. The fly would float easily on the modest bankside current for a couple of feet before a set of white jaws opened on the surface and engulfed the fake. Then all hell would break loose with the fish leaping, splashing and diving down deep while shaking its head. Brought to hand, Ginny admired the trout before swiftly releasing the fish, which disappeared into the darkness with a couple of flicks of its thick caudal fin. I admired her and took a number of photos of the action. A couple of times our canine companion would swim out to the struggling trout and try to follow its madcap antics about the side channel. Once the line zipped underneath him and the friction snapped the delicate leader. Realizing what he'd done, Bouchee came to shore some feet below us, shook himself and watched our actions with a sincere look of remorse that seemed to say "Sorry, guys. I won't do that again." Ginny put down her rod, went over to him and rubbed his ears and cooed compliments about his lineage and behavior. He was soon back in the river, though downstream of where we were fishing scrounging for rocks that he brought to the shore in his dripping jaws. In no time he'd accumulated a pile of the stones that looked like a cairn marking our day's activities. He dropped down in the grey sand and looked out upon his world with extreme satisfaction. For now the world was his to enjoy.

The smoke had cleared off somewhat. The sky now

appeared a shade of washed out blue and the sun, still high in the west, was yellow-orange, shielded enough in the haze that you could look directly at it without blinking or temporarily blinding yourself. The fishing had been excellent to put things mildly, so we decided to call a halt to the angling proceedings, head back and have our lunch. The dog, with visions of food on his mind, was already running along back down the ranch road well ahead of us, nose tight to the ground with still other visions of sharp-tailed grouse in his mind. Roast beef sandwiches, kosher dill pickles, peach pie, some iced tea and, since she loved Cuban cigars, a couple of La Gloria Cubana Medaille d'Or No. 4s. Not bad for a derelict writer slash fly fisher – a wonderful woman companion, my buddy Bouchee in fine form, great fishing and superb food and cigars. I realized that I both wanted and understood that I needed more of this life. Living inside my head while writing novels or any other verbal crap for that matter, made it quite easy to slip into extreme narrow mindedness and joy-killing cynicism. No way I wanted any more of that noise.

    The lunch was excellent. The roast beef roasted to medium-rare perfection on homemade sour dough bread was simple and absurdly good. The rest of the feast was equally good. The dog devoured about a pound of the beef, belched and collapsed into instant sleep. We put things away, sat back with our cigars and sipped iced tea. My kind of life.

    "Where do you come up with these," asked Ginny. "This is absolutely one of the best tasting, most floral scented cigars I've ever had. A girl like me could chain smoke and inhale these little beauties."

    "I wouldn't advise it. You'd be dead in a couple of months."

    "Kill joy."

Road Fish

"Yeah, I know. Life is to be lived to its fullest and the road of excess leads to the palace of wisdom and all that jive," I said.

"All very true as long as practiced with a hint of moderation."

"Moderation has not and never will be part of my life," I said. "I'm serious here. I'm either all in or all out. That's how it works for me."

"I saw that in you when we met at Jake's in Whitefish years ago," Ginny said as she leaned towards me. "To recognize this in yourself puts you somewhat ahead of the self- righteous, delusional nitwits dashing around spouting their PC nonsense. You seem to have made some progress over the years. But enough of this. Let's go back to being self-indulgent kids."

I agreed. God! It was easy to climb up on a soapbox. A classic example of bullshit calling out bullshit. Ginny agreed and poured us some more tea. We then talked of this and that including a place Ginny knew of where I could pick up a couple of well-seasoned cords of aspen from a logger who frequented a local store. At only $120 a cord this was a very good deal.

~ ~ ~

When Black Friday comes
I'll stand down by the door
And catch the grey men when they
Dive from the fourteenth floor

When the opening chords on the piano breezed through my speakers as I headed east up I90 from Missoula to Rock Creek one morning in 1975 I knew that I'd tumbled onto new and unique road music. As *Black Friday* glided into *Bad Sneakers* ...

And I'm going insane
And I'm laughing at the frozen rain

John Holt

And I'm so alone
Honey when they gonna send me home

The Montana weather turned to sleet. I drank from a bottle of Taylor's Champagne and realized that Steely Dan had found a place in my road life. Their stuff wasn't rock and it wasn't jazz but a blend of all of the contemporary sound back then. By the time *Daddy Don't Live In That New York City No More...*

He can't get tight every night
 Pass out on the barroom floor

... the stereo was blasting full tilt. The weather turned to cold rain and the dirt road along the stream was greasy, so I said the hell with the fishing and pulled over along Valley of the Moon. Listening to the tape as it looped back on its self, smoking Camel straights, drinking the wine and watching the water dance in the snow was plenty.

Forty years later I bought a CD copy of *Katy Lied* and listened to the music as I rolled east out of Livingston, again on I90 but this time around beside the Yellowstone heading for a side channel near Reed Point. Those same piano chords made 1975 seem like yesterday. Becker and Fagen tripped me back to free-form times while seamlessly blending with contemporary interstate motion as I cruised past Big Timber then Grey Cliff.

Steely Dan's produced a lot of great music since 1975 but nothing works like *Katy Lied* when it comes to dragging an old freak back to his chaotic youth while he staggers along in the modern world. It's all there – the delusions, illusions, the sweet lies that bleed us all and most wonderfully, the dreams. I don't mind being in my sixties and I didn't mind being twenty-four in Missoula. Steely Dan's ability to draw me into to both

Road Fish

times and others simultaneously is right there with a real fine mescaline buzz. I've wondered as I've driven into the Missouri Breaks or up along the Hi-line while Doctor Wu played if Becker and Fagen saw their sixties when they wrote these songs.

Are you crazy are you high
Or just an ordinary guy ...

After many years of wandering badly while chasing trout, northerns, goldeye, pygmy catfish or whatever, I've caught fish enough to now be more entranced with the stream and its surroundings than anything else. Catching a lot of fish or even a few truly big ones isn't important anymore. The take, the fight, the beauty of the quarry is more than all right, but not all encompassing. Just spending time on a beautiful little mountain river in mid-April with a good, albeit slightly crazy, friend is more than enough. Surviving another winter and playing outside with a fly rod once again after a very long winter on any stream always seems miraculous to me, like being a kid once again still filled with naïve and optimistic expectations. This is joyfully unlike those slight intimations of approaching gloom that are admittedly part of what makes late-October glorious when fishing for big browns. But that experience is sometimes cerebrally shaded with a soundtrack like Sinatra's rendering of *It Was A Very Good Year*, the autumn of my life part.

We walked downstream a mile or so in under a partly cloudy sky the air pine scented in the spring warmth. We fished our way up with small attractors, Yellow Humpies, Royal Wullfs and such. I didn't catch anything. My friend caught two small Yellowstone cutthroat. He decided to sit on a gravel bank, smoke a cigar and enjoy the sunny day. I chose to move upstream beneath a bridge and on into a forested, canyon-like stretch that I'd never fished, but thought, "What the hell? Why Not?" I changed to a stouter tippet and tied on a Cree-Hackled Bugger, a pattern I've been using for decades. Weighted with a little bit of shot pinched on at the head, I was in a search-cast-and-take-no-prisoners mode, flinging the Bugger into any promising run, pool or tight against brush-covered banks.

Following a bunch of artfully presented casts that produced nothing, I pushed through bankside trees and brush sliding over moss-covered rocks until I reach the tail of the deep aquamarine run that really wanted to be a pool. I launched the Bugger 40 feet just below where the current gushed through a gash in a large slab of rock. The pattern sunk rapidly and rushed towards me as I stripped line to maintain contact. Just as I began lifting for another cast a trout surged just below the surface and engulfed the Bugger setting the hook itself. Pulling back the rod bent and pulsed as the fish torpedoed taking line with a buzz of the reel and then circled the parameters of the pool. In a minute it came to hand, a very large Yellowstone cutthroat, muted spring shadings gone silvery from those vibrant spawning colors of last year. The throat slashes were red-orange and an inch or so long. I marked it against my rod and later taped this – 21 inches, maybe three pounds. By far the biggest cutthroat I'd ever taken in this stream.

Quite odd I thought and moved 20 yards upstream to water that was nearly identical. Another cast to the top of the run, another deep drift and another embryonic lift of the rod to cast and again something big hit the fly. The thrashing repeated itself and quickly a nearly identical westslope was marked against the rod – same length – and released.

Truly odd.

Road Fish

The water above me shallowed as it splayed out over gravel streambed, so I returned to my friend who was finishing his cigar. When I told him what happened, he said, "That's odd. We need to come back after runoff." At times he's a friend of few words. We both agreed that the two big trout were an unexpected occurrence, especially way up here.

When I look back on this I guess it's simply a case of "Odd is as odd does."

~ ~ ~

The noise was loud. Somebody needed to shut up those damn birds. Screw Sandhill cranes. And at the moment, the hell with this dandy, little brown trout stream. And while we're at it, the hell with April springtime in Montana. I rolled out from beneath my Toyota pickup, a bottle of Jim Beam and a few cans of Pabst clattering together in the waxed-cotton coat. The grass was wet from the rain. Ground fog obscured the large birds clacking away in a muddy field on the other side of the river. No sun through the overcast. I guessed a little short of six. I took a long pull of the Beam, draining the bottle and tossed it into the truck's bed. The metallic clatter stopped the cranes for a moment. I drained two cans of beer. Dehydration blues. Tossed them into the back. They didn't make as much noise. Drained the few ounces left in another bottle of whiskey and tossed it, too. Glass shattered and the birds quieted again, longer this time. I still had eight bottles of whiskey from the case I'd purchased a few days before. No need to drive into Harlowton. I was starting to feel all right again. The Sandhills were cool now. I had a three- to four-hour window where I could reasonably function in terms of wading, casting and catching fish. Then, with a little luck, I'd stagger back to the truck, rig the tent, spread the sleeping bag, build a fire, drink more Jim Beam, and pass out until the evening rise. Routines are reassuring, especially for someone who lives to drink.

The year could have been anyone from 1963 (I got an early start) to 2007. They were all slight variations of a predictable theme. Vices, addictions, bad habits. Fuck it. I liked to drink. That's all. No fancy b.s. to explain away boorish behavior or justify my full-tilt madness. I just plain old liked to get hammered twenty-four hours a day, all the time. The predictability and the attendant boredom of the experience eventually made saying so long to the booze easy. Damn easy. But I never take this easiness for granted. When something bores me I'm gone. So what if the mediocre epiphany took more than four decades. Swilling enough liquor to feel like master of the universe then inevitable transition into a repetitive, babbling blackout drunk. I'd say anything to anyone, though I never remembered a word. I did remember some the words the next time I spoke to these often unaware victims of my verbal onslaught. I was called, justly I figure, all kinds of dirty names and often described in terms that made my prodigious turns of phrase seem puny. When I quit I also gave up all sorts of drugs and even cigarettes. Just to keep my hand in, a gentle soul such as myself does need one vice to clutch dearly to his breast, I became passionate about cigars. Not just any cigars, the best I can find. This minor, though not inexpensive, bad habit and extremely enjoyable pursuit fills the void that the self-absorbed career of being a hardcore sodden maniac once occupied. The smoke keeps me happy.

I'm grateful. I don't miss the booze in the least. God blessed me on this one.

(*Author's note: For a more involved examination of "the life" I recommend two novels by the late John O'Brien – The Assault on Tony's and Leaving Las*

Road Fish

Vegas. In 1994 two weeks after O'Brien was informed that Leaving Las Vegas was going to be made into a movie, he shot himself. He was 33. His father later said that the novel was O'Brien's suicide note.)

~ ~ ~

The high-summer terrestrial fishing on the side channels of the river that flowed through our town had been excellent to say the least. As dusk came on we switched from hopper patterns, mainly Joe's, to a cricket tied in similar fashion but in black shades of life. We could hear the sounds of the bugs chirping in the bankside grasses, a sound that brought us back to the fields of our long-ago Midwestern youths. As we readied to make our casts to several large trout that were lined up along the near bank feeding on the crickets in grasshopper fashion, Ginny nudged my arm and said softly, "Look at that," as she pointed to a shallow section of the main river no more than 100 yards upstream.

In the now grey light turning white-silver from the glow cast by a rising and waxing three-quarter-full moon a long string of white-tails begin crossing the Yellowstone bound for the hay fields on the far shore. In no time the herd stretched from the willow-covered island across a broad gravel bar through the river and well into the lush grass. This went on for minutes. When completed there must have been 200 deer browsing in the field. Neither of us had ever seen anything like it, at least not in such large numbers.

More magic on the stream. We passed on the fishing and returned to camp and the runout of the side channel we'd been working all day, rebuilt the fire, sat back and took in the site of hundreds of deer, the light and sound of our fire and the feel of velvet air of a July evening in a damn nice setting.

CHAPTER FOURTEEN
West Boulder Fire Aftermath –
Torched Forest Belies Healthy Stream

THERE ARE TIMES WHEN FLY FISHING for trout, northerns, smallmouth or the noble goldeye takes on slightly bizarre, eerie shadings. Many of these occasions are out of kilter not because the taking of the fish is exceptionally easy or extremely difficult but because of other circumstances. Weird light. Strange humans wandering around on the periphery of my vision. Grizzly vibes humming electrically through the land. Today is one of those moments that even when viewed from this distance of several months seems to be a still-life study of some monumental truth that I can only glimpse along the outer boundaries of perception. It's like I'm wearing a ball cap (Cubs normally) and the bill is pulled down over my eyes so that all I can see is the ground directly beneath me at my feet and a little beyond. I know that there's more to the landscape but I can't glimpse it. Frustrating. A touch maddening.

    I'm casting to Yellowstone cutthroat in the wide oxbows and flats of the West Boulder River in the meadows section in the Absaroka-Beartooth Wilderness about four miles up from the trailhead. At first the hike coursed through a healthy forest of pine and aspen. Alder and willow lined the banks of the free-stone stream. Ravens and magpies called among themselves. After crossing a wooden bridge over the West Boulder the trail switched backed its way up several hundred feet before running along the side of a burned over slope. Trees were devoid of needles, trunks blackened. Many had toppled and were lying

Road Fish

corpse-like in the soil turned washed-out red from the heat of the fire. The view was still excellent. Mountains covered in fresh snow on their upper reaches crowded the horizon in the south, east and west. Behind me I could see far out to the Yellowstone Valley. Farther north, the tops of the Crazies were visible, strings of light cloud clinging to their summits. Soon the meadows and the sparking water of the West Boulder came into sight and all awareness of the charcoal shaded surroundings was replaced with an eagerness to rig up and cast to the cutthroat that even from this height were making visible rise forms. I dropped down the steep trail to the valley, waded through the thick sere gray-yellow grasses to the bank. The grasses were still waist high but not the rich green shoulder height growth of July when reaching the water bears some resemblance to a jungle safari.

    I begin casting along dense mats of weed, next to brushy banks or out in the middle of the clear blue to cruising fish. The wind is up so some allowances were made for its gusting effects on the line.

    The trout eagerly grab a Gold-ribbed hare's ear nymph or casually take a #14 tan Elk Hair caddis. The fish fight in a series of gradually shorter deep runs before thrashing their heads as they came to me. The cutthroat are all over twelve inches. Some more than sixteen. Fat, healthy. Radiating the purest of colors – orange, emerald, crimson, black, white, gold, bronze. Natural perfection. The day is early autumn gorgeous featuring a cloudless blue sky, temperature in the seventies and the fluctuating wind was warm and smelled of water, the grass and distant snowfields. The West Boulder Plateau dominates the eastern horizon. Mount Cowan at 11,206 feet holds sway in the southern distance. The northern boundary of Yellowstone National Park is another twenty miles in the same direction. Sheer cliffs of convoluted rock that is tinted ochre rise along the western skyline, their faces pockmarked with large cave openings. Everything seems as it should be. Like it always has been whenever I've visited in the past, but something seems odd, out of place.

The obvious frequently eludes me for a variety of marginally explainable reasons that aren't worth going into here. This elusion connects with the bizarre strings attached to life, and the obvious in this case is the fact that the dense, deep-green carpeting of pine forest that normally surrounds the stream dropping down to the valley floor is gone. In its place stand thousands upon thousands of blackened pine skeletons and burned out hulks of trunks. This battlefield of the dead trees resembles that of their brothers and sisters I'd passed on the way in here. So focused on the stream and the fishing and the notion that even with the devastation of the fires of 2006 this radically altered landscape remains spectacular, high country beautiful, I'd blocked the carnage from my awareness. Look the other way, Holt and everything bad will go away. Childish self-absorption surfacing in clear air.

~ ~ ~

In the fire year that was 2006 the West Boulder flames blazed away razing tens of thousands of acres of prime forest on both public and private land. Wildlife and livestock were incinerated. Homes were lost. The air was clogged with soot and ash miles away in my hometown of Livingston. The yard looked grayish green from the fall of particulate. On occasions when the smoldering areas blew up the column of smoke resembled a mushroom cloud that rose far into the sky before being leveled out by the southwest wind that pushed the mess towards the Dakotas. At night the clouds often glowed with an orange internal fire reflecting the firestorm at their bases. Firefighters reported seeing tornados of fire ripping through the timber. Crown fires raced across treetops.

The fire, started by lightning Aug. 25, 2006, was on the West Boulder River about 30 miles north of Yellowstone National Park. The 2006 fire season ranked among the worst ever. Right up there with those of 1988, 2000 and 2003.

"We are seeing fire behavior in the past week that no one has ever seen before," Bill Avey, a district ranger in Big Timber for the Gallatin National Forest, said at the time.

When I'd wake up in the morning during late-summer days of dead heat, when I'd walk around town, when I'd go to bed at night, smoke was all around me, burning my eyes, filling my lungs, and obscuring my vision some days so that I couldn't see the Crazy Mountains only twenty miles away during my daily strolls along the banks of Yellowstone River. There were wildfires burning everywhere – wildfires burning in the southwestern part of the state nearly 200 miles away over several mountain ranges, wildfires burning 300 miles away in the northwest corner of Montana, wildfires in Wyoming and Idaho, and much of the smoke, it seems, converged here in town. Many people in other locations felt the same thing on this front.

When the air was still everything in town looked like it was cloaked in singed fog.

Forest fires in the West are a natural phenomenon. They occur every year and sometimes, like in 1988, they blow up and scorch hundreds of thousands of acres of spectacular country, as they did in Yellowstone National Park back then.

That's the natural way of it out here, especially in

years of low to average snowpack, drought and high heat, and in the long run it does more good than harm—or so I tell myself. Then I call my Mom in Whitefish in the Flathead Valley by Glacier National Park and quite close to the fires raging over there.

"It's nothing but smoke over here," says Mom. "First the floods of several years ago, now this every summer. What's next? Hordes of locusts? Last night was spooky. Around six it was like dusk. The smoke turned the sun into a dull, orange ball. I haven't seen the mountains in weeks. I can stare directly at the sun all day. It's just a blood red ball up in the sky. The smoke and the never-ending heat – it's like hell."

I thought about natural process, the firefighter, and my mother one afternoon as I walked through the smoky haze along the Yellowstone one stifling hot afternoon. The water level was as low as I'd ever seen it, caused by the drought and ranchers sucking water out of the riverine system for yet another cut of hay. The nearby Shields and Musselshell Rivers were less than a trickle for the same reasons and closed to fishing as were many streams in the state. Those not completely closed required anglers to be off the water by 2 p.m.

Many of us were counting on the August Singularity arriving on schedule near the end of the month as it always has in Montana in the past. This first cool sweep of moisture wandering down from northern Canada normally brings with it a couple of days of light, though steady rain, enough to cleanse the air and slow the fires until the snows of late September.

All of these walls of flame and immense columns of smoke with firefighters battling in the foreground while residents flee with few if any possessions in a chaotic cavalcade of pickups, vans and cars makes for

Road Fish

a great 32-second visual bite on the nightly network news, but it's a lot different when that crown fire races through the tree tops at over 60 miles-an-hour, flames spinning and roaring in those glowing, orange tornados hundreds of feet high that are thundering down on your home. The scene is intoxicating on TV, but it's terrifying to experience firsthand, and for those of us who try to live through all of it, it's hell.

When the rains of September finally came and put an end to the inferno madness fires in Montana burned more than 800,000 acres, over 300 homes, and caused millions of dollars in damage. What was unusual was that the largest fires occurred east of the Continental Divide – the 191,000-acre Derby Mountain fire southeast of Big Timber, the Pine Ridge fire east of Billings that charred 121,210 acres, the Black Pulaski Complex that burned some 124,000 acres in central Montana, and the Bundy Railroad fire south of Billings that burned more than 91,000 acres.

Fishing friends that I spoke with expressed concern about the health, even survival, of native trout populations in affected drainages like the West Boulder. "How could anything live through all of this?" they'd say. It was a good question. Next year would tell the story.

~ ~ ~

Wildfires, while destroying much in their paths, can also generate benefits. Many plants reappear quickly following wildfires, because fire converts organic matter to available mineral nutrients. Some plant species, such as aspen and many native grasses re-grow from root systems that are rarely damaged by wildfire. Other plant species, such as lodgepole pine and jack pine, have evolved to depend on stand replacement fires for their regeneration; fire is necessary to open their cones and spread the seeds.

Some ecosystems are even threatened by fire exclusion including aspen, whitebark pine, and Ponderosa pine (western montane ecosystems), and the tallgrass prairie. Research has revealed that of the 146 rare, threatened, or endangered plants in the lower 48 states for which there is conclusive information on fire effects, 135 species (92%) benefit from fire or are found in fire-adapted ecosystems.

Animals, as well as plants, can benefit from fire. Some individual animals are killed, especially by catastrophic fires, but populations and communities are rarely threatened. Many species are attracted to burned areas following fires — some even during or immediately after the fire. Species can be attracted by the newly available minerals or the reduced vegetation allowing them to see and catch prey. Others are attracted in the growth including fresh and available seeds and berries, for insects and other prey or for habitat. A few may be highly dependent on fire; the endangered Kirtland's warbler only nests under young jack pine that is regenerated by fire, because only these types of jack pine stands are dense enough to protect the nestlings from predators.

The ecological benefits of wildfires often outweigh their negative effects which include loss of canopy cover, soil erosion, siltation, habitat loss for numerous species of birds, mammals, fish, plants and insects, and sometimes the release of heavy metals exposed by the blazes into water systems. A regular occurrence of fires can reduce the amount of fuel build-up thereby lowering the likelihood of a potentially large wildfire. Fires often remove alien plants that compete with native species for nutrients and space, and remove undergrowth, which allows sunlight to reach the forest floor, thereby supporting the growth of native species.

The ashes that remain after a fire add nutrients

often locked in older vegetation to the soil for trees and other vegetation. Fires can also provide a way for controlling insect pests by killing off the older or diseased trees and leaving the younger, healthier trees. Burned trees provide habitat for nesting birds, homes for mammals and a nutrient base for new plants. When these trees decay, they return even more nutrients to the soil. Overall, fire is a catalyst for promoting biological diversity and healthy ecosystems. It fosters new plant growth and wildlife populations often expand as a result.

~ ~ ~

So I am surprised and pleased that this small section of paradise was still intact. Changed to be sure. Sadly missing the greens of the pine forest and the fall brilliance of the copses of aspen, but still a viable system. Grasshoppers leap with suicidal vehemence onto the water. The Yellowstones slurp them down with a carefree gluttony that only cutthroats exhibit. I can't resist casting to them over and over. I tie on a Cree-hackled Woolly bugger and launch the thing out into the middle of a large bend in the river. It lands with a splashy "plop" and begins to sink. I watch as the pattern moves through the water column. Dozens of trout ride in on the bugger. They flash and swirl around it. They make menacing gestures and bat it with their heads and tails. Finally a large one, maybe 18 inches, has had enough. White mouth wide open the Yellowstone engulfs and heads for cover. I lift up on the rod quickly to set the hook before the bugger goes too far in. The cutthroat is stunned and runs about in erratic circles for a minute before tiring and coming to shore. The colors of this one are intense almost to the level of fluorescence. The hook twists easily from its upper jaw. The fish quivers from one end of its body to the other then shoots down to the depths and vanishes from my site. This last cutthroat is enough. I'm finished (have been for some years, actually). I look about me taking in the still-very-much-alive scene. A couple of late-season Western Tiger Swallowtail butterflies glide and loop above the grass. A group of mallards swoop low overhead wings out and arched for landing. The drakes' emerald necks glisten in the sunlight. The mountains rising everywhere are still majestic. The sky holds a few clouds whose shadows glide across the ground. And I realize that next spring a fresh wave of bright green plants including the beginnings of the new forest will light up the countryside in the meadows of the West Boulder River.

CHAPTER FIFTEEN
Fencing the Sky

... I suspect that men are going along this way for the last time, and I for one don't want to waste the trip ...
— Robert Traver, *Anatomy of a Fisherman*

MY DIFFICULTIES WITH FENCES began some years ago, a delicate transmutation arising from problems I had and still have with gates. Either my hands get scratched from trying to latch the ragged compilations of weathered tree limbs and barbed wire that block passage to some exotic fishing water or I pinch my fingers in the workings of the newer hook-type mechanism or I become inextricably tangled in the wire while crossing through. And with the certainty of an eastern-horizon sunrise, I find myself on the wrong sides of these gates after closing them. Coming or going, it doesn't matter. The Suburban is always beyond the gate waiting for me to figure things out.

When I turned sixty crossing fences turned into a struggle. I'm in fairly good shape, not too much overweight, and manage to totter around with a modest degree of authority, but now I cannot get over, under or through a fence, particularly barbed wire ones, without some sort of mishap. All of the shirts I wear fishing are torn along the shoulders and back. My sweaters have loops pulled from their tight knitting large enough to hold ice axes, and my waders leak, doing little more now than visually announce that I'm about to chase some fish.

One time along the Shields River I became entangled while stooping and grunting through some

Road Fish

wire that silently guarded a delightful stretch of prime water. Frustrated, I could hear trout splashing after caddis less than 30 feet away- I jerked free only to have the tip guide of my fly rod hook on a rusty barb. Jerking the rod sharply I lost my footing, the rod separating at midsection. I slid to the bottom of the embankment with line humming off the reel as though I'd hooked a five-pound brown. Nothing serious came of this calamity. I lost a few minutes of my life during regrouping. The tip guide was bent into a narrow oval and my torn shirt was now more torn. I was dusty and bedraggled, but that's how I wind up looking after fishing anyway. I went on to have a pleasant day catching a few browns, but that incident was the beginning of my firm dislike for fences and a beginning of an awareness concerning our obsession with closing land in, delineating, and not so tacitly stating that, a given piece of property that is owned is now no longer a part of what's left of free range in the West.

We're all obsessed with possession. Relationships between the sexes are often defined by the scars of these emotional turf wars. That's to be expected. We're a flawed species. And purchasing a piece of land is overt possession, but controlling this land is absurd. Yeah, I understand that if someone pays the bucks they can do what they want with the acreage. Cattle must be managed. And riffraff such as myself needs to be kept at bay. A dwindling few ranchers still allow access to their land if a person politely asks and remembers to thank them with a Christmas bottle of rye whiskey or such. But the whole ownership thing is out of control on the high plains. Orange spray-painted fence posts by the millions, "Keep Out" signs swaying in the wind and "No hunting or fishing. No trespassing" warnings. How a person can do the former two without committing the latter is a mystery.

This variation seems a case of restating the obvious. If you can't pass, you logically can't fish or hunt.

And I love the entrances to many of the newer ranches or ranchettes, the ones marked by a pair of enormous rotting Ponderosa pine trunks topped by an equally large trunk across the top. And dangling below the top brace in clear examples of human hauteur are signs that dance to the tune of "Smith's Ponderosa" or "Letterman's Wild West Haven" or, my personal favorite, "Wall Street Retreat." Thankfully the plains Indians never adopted this insecure form of territorialism. Visions of "Plenty Coups' Palace" or "Dull Knife's Estancia" come shakily to mind.

All of this makes sense to me. Let's all hem in the land and its spirit with miles of barbed wire and then announce to the world who exactly is responsible for this self-absorbed mayhem. Like we own the good country in the long term. Recent wildfires in Montana and now California say otherwise, as do drought, earthquake and the inevitable ice age. I've never been a wannabe Indian. Not my style, and quite sensibly on the tribes' part, they don't want me, but whatever happened to respecting the land that can never be truly owned? What about honoring and submitting to the long-running buzz that is the electric spirit of the West?

Sure fencing one's property ensures at least the illusion of privacy and security. We can all drive down our private, dusty lanes, sit on the front porch and arrogantly say while sipping some expensive single malt, "I've got mine. You can't have it. I'm really living now." The mentality that made us great hideously guts the essence of open space.

Up until a few years ago I couldn't imagine what Montana or the Dakotas would have been like 150 years ago. A land of no fences, few people and a

Road Fish

vastness filled with wild animals that rivaled Africa's now ravaged Serengeti. Some years back I'd been drifting up to the far north of the Yukon and Northwest Territories with increasing frequency while researching a book. When I first drove through the hundreds of miles of uncut boreal forest and crossed rivers like the Mackenzie that are more than a mile wide and 40 feet deep, when I saw thousands of woodland bison grazing by the dirt roads that are called highways up there, I was blown away. To finally experience such an immense wealth of wilderness, an area many times the size of Montana, with so few signs of people was staggering. To catch countless grayling of several pounds from one small stretch of river was stunning. One day as I cruised up to the First Nations Dene De Cho settlement of Pedzah Ki, I watched the Mackenzie flow, not flow but power, its way north to above the Arctic Circle and finally into the Beaufort Sea. The Canyon Range, then the Mackenzie Range, then other mountains rolled away to the west for hundreds of miles. Moose ghosted through stands of dwarf birch. Black bears were all over the place feeding on the green, rich grasses of a short, intense summer. Through binoculars I sighted grizzlies wandering the slopes of the McConnell Range. Fifty miles to the south, Nahanni Butte shimmered silvery blue. For days I saw only a few settlements of maybe 100 people each. No phone or electric lines. No fences. The difference in the energy, in the feel, of this land was palpable. The countryside sizzled and seemed to flicker with a light that is not seen by the eyes. This must have been what the Big Sky felt like a couple of centuries past. Montana is home in my heart, but the North in its, for now, untamed radiance owns my soul.

    Experiencing all of this up north made me see that we don't improve things for ourselves or, more importantly, for the good country when we attempt to stamp our designs of control on the landscape. Instead we cut out the heart of the place and in the process slice away chunks of ourselves. Someday Ginny and I may move out of Livingston and back into the empty, open spaces. I'd like to believe that we'll tear down all of the fences on whatever place we find, but knowing myself, I doubt it. We want our piece of paradise just like anyone else.

    Last October while returning from another day fishing on the Shields I crossed several fences on the way back to the Suburban. Angus cattle were casually grazing on the last of the year's good grass. As is normal these days, I fought with a fence near the highway. When I finally passed through I looked up and saw a lone cow standing on the roadside of the fence. Cattle do this. They always want what they see on the other side, then decide that they really need to return to their original side of the obstruction. The animal was pushing against the barbed wire trying to rejoin its herd. The cow bawled in its frustration. A large gash ran along its flank. Blood from the wound glistened in the sunlight. I turned away, unlocked the back doors of the rig and started to put away my gear. I looked down at my right hand. A long scratch ran from the base of the little finger to the wrist. There was a good deal of blood that, too, glistened in the light.

CHAPTER SIXTEEN
Wild Life –
Autumn High Plains Fishing

I'm goin' up on the mountain
Find me uh cave 'n talk the bears
In t' takin' me in
Wild life is uh mans best friend
                         - *Wild Life* by Captain Beefheart
                                from *Trout Mask Replica*

THE CRASH OF METAL DOORS clangs through the still late-September afternoon air. The sound of a diesel truck engine starting followed by a rough grinding noise as the gears are engaged follows. An old Dodge Power Wagon slowly appears moving from right to left through a background of sage flats and rolling hills. The rusted, grey truck begins winding down a gravel road pulling an equally rusted horse trailer that was once white. Patches of yellowing paint bear this out. I follow the machine's progress as it lugs away from me by watching the black exhaust that rises above a line of old cottonwoods along the road. The smoke climbs into the sky accompanying the sound of the struggling Dodge, seeming as though an old Baldwin steam locomotive pulling empty cattle cars is shuffling along some abandoned and invisible rail line.

    The racket fades to nothing. All I'm left with is the rustling of leaves and the burbling of cool, clear water over the copper-colored streambed at my feet. I've been working my way up this stream using a #14 Tan Humpy that takes Yellowstone cutthroat, brook and a couple of fat brown trout. Lots of fish, some missed,

Road Fish

some not. I know that just up ahead in a slight depression beneath a brushy overhang there is a brown trout. There always is. Fifteen, eighteen, twenty inches. Depends on the year and finally the season. I dry the fly by squeezing it in my shirt, then gauge the cast to a spot several feet above the hold, enough distance to gain slight contact with the bug and throw a small upstream bend in the line a little above the butt of the leader.

Out of nothing but solitude a roar and stomping erupts from the field above and to the left. Bellowing so loud it crackles in my ears like a low-flying F16. Hooves pound the earth with a ferocity that thrums into my gut. Clouds of brown dirt, manure and grass erupt above the yellowing bankside grasses. An angry animal. This goes on for a long time, maybe a couple of minutes. I recall Ken Kesey's wonderful short story *Abdul & Ebenezer*, but before I wander down that long-ago road I'm distracted by a similar ruckus to right of me. Again out of sight of where my position in the water below banks of six feet or so. Another bull roars and smashes mad feet at the ground. I can't see the dirt this time though I hear it raining down on leaves and grass.

Neither animal moves and I sense that they are facing each other in a bovine version of a turf war. I visualize necks bulging, thick tails swishing back and forth like deadly quirts wielded by insane Mongols, thick drool falling from foaming mouths arced in savage snarls as the slimy stuff forms dark puddles of mud beneath hooves resembling anvils that rip the ground on either sides of their enormous heads. I look up and see three ravens streaking silently off towards the Crazies. The birds know when to leave a scene turned unexpectedly primal.

I wait and marvel at the mayhem swirling around

me. This is both exciting and terrifying. What if these enraged beasts thunder towards each other and find me standing in the way of their combativeness? I'll probably be gored and smashed into bloody mush. I look at the slender 6-foot-six-inch bamboo rod in my right hand and flash on it smashed, the splintered strips floating downstream on a bubbling, crimson froth. I should turn around and quietly take my leave, except that there's a real dilemma here. I watch the depression in the streambed, the one protected by the brushy overhang. A brown of size is grabbing caddis as they whirl their way upwards into the bending grass. I want to fool this trout.

    As has been the case once already in the early going of this autumn, the fishing is broaching the arresting side of life.

~ ~ ~

    I've looked for this stretch of river in central Montana for more than thirty years, temporarily quitting the hunt in the late nineties to pursue new water that is easier to find. For some reason I'd never come across this wild place that a long-ago acquaintance said held small numbers of enormous brown trout. Five pounds was considered average in this gentlemen's estimation. He told me this while banging back shots of bar whiskey at a bar in Jordan. A stub of a cheap Garcia y Vega claro cigar (the band was still on the thing) wedged in a corner of his mouth. We talked and drank for a while and I gathered as much information as I could from the guy such as use the "biggest damn fly" I had "down on the bottom." He called a halt to the proceedings by downing one last shot, pushing away from the bar and out the door into the rain. Never saw him gain. Gravel roads, little used state roads, two tracks – I'd run down and around a lot of them often more than once with no success. Perhaps

Road Fish

this was due to a combination of whiskey, beer and a general condition of geographical confusion regarding the region in question during those chaotic days of yesteryear. And yes, things are so much clearer now.

But today I'd driven straight to the river like I'd fished it all my life. No wrong turns. No confusion. The last stretch of road was abandoned pavement marked by a large barricade that said "Local traffic only!" The exclamation point lent an element of danger to the process. About a mile ahead the byway abruptly ended with another barricade leaning precariously to the edge of the macadam. No sign this time. The results of proceeding any further were obvious. One-hundred yards of the slope on the south side had slumped down towards the river taking the road with it. The landside surged down the steep incline and stopped well short of the river. This must have happened some time ago. Sage, weeds and some rough grass grew from the displaced material. I stopped the Suburban. Set the brake. Grabbed my binoculars and walked to the edge of the incline right above the slump that was thousands of cubic yards in size.

Before I could start glassing the setting a late-model white Dodge pick-up turned up my way from a two-track exiting a barren field. As the truck drove slowly by two red-faced gentleman stared at me, took long drinks from cans of Ranier, laughed with what appeared sodden sincerity and drove off. It was nice to know that I wasn't completely alone.

The binoculars brought the river to me in clear relief, crystal detail. The water flowed darkly across a wide gravel and rock-strewn bar braiding into a number of deep green channels for perhaps a half-mile. Deadfalls, limbs and brush was piled along the various seams' path or partially embedded in the gravel making ideal holding water for large fish.

Further down the braids merged, the current then wandering like an anaconda (tunes from Joni Mitchell's *The Hissing of Summer Lawns* drifted along the airwaves) against cutbanks and grassy fields filled with large cottonwoods that leaned over the river. Some, having succumbed to the erosive intent of the water, lay partially submerged at various angles of recline along the way creating still more holding water. The river disappeared around a bend beneath a sharp cliff made up of seams of limestone, clay, shale and coal that formed a pale geologic rainbow before disappearing into the southern beginnings of the Missouri Breaks. Despite being near roads and ranches this land felt wild and untouched. The spookiness of the Breaks was out there shimmering in the near distance. I looked back up the road and saw a barbed-wire gate that was pulled open and left lying in the ditch. I'd park up there tomorrow and walk across a stubble field and down through a coulee for a mile or so then through the cottonwoods and brush to the river. A pair of Red-tails glided above a slight ridge beyond the gate. The air smelled of dry land and juniper. There were clumps of the bushes scattered about on the southern sides of the hills.

  The day was windy with high overcast. Darker weather was boiling up behind this in the west when I'd first stopped to examine the country twenty minutes ago. I returned to the Suburban to head back to town. Topping the rise I looked back in that direction of the storm and saw a dark wall of cloud closing fast behind me. Beneath the middle of the rotating storm a large rectangular shape formed in seconds. Small vertical spirals of dark froth ripped out from the edges. A roaring began that sounded like a bunch of enormous fans set on high speed, the kind used for special effects in the movies when hurricanes

Road Fish

are needed. A funnel cloud appeared. In an instant it was there maybe 700 yards from the Suburban. No protracted formation like the videos on TV where the tornado reaches towards the ground while a similar shape reaches up to join its twin. The cloud shelf above it started to spin and form spiral shapes like full-curl ram's horns. I opened the door. Actually it was sucked away from my hand by the inflow to the tornado. The vortex blasted across the far bench above the river, extended down into the narrow valley sucking grass, leaves and water, maybe even the big browns, as it crossed, before bouncing up the near rise to the south turning from tan to blue-grey as it did so. Wind swirled around in crazy gusts coming from all directions before coalescing and racing off to the east in waves that alternated from cold to warm to cold. The funnel pushed southeast contrary to the northeast direction I'd seen tornados move in the past in other parts of the state. Within minutes the twister was hidden behind dark sheets of moisture that drenched everything including me in a wash of icy water more torrential downpour than rain.

    The weather rolled away leaving behind a ceiling of low lead-colored clouds. I returned to my motel room for a hot shower, a hot meal and a warm bed. I'd examined the cable guide when I checked in earlier today. Two weird movies are scheduled– *After...* and *Monsters*. I was set for the night. I'd be back here chasing the rumored browns in the morning.

    The next day I was at the river by 10 a.m. The air was warming already with a partly cloudy sky and a light wind from the southwest. On my walk in here I'd crossed a small spring-fed creek that raced down the coulee below alongside of the dirt road that lead to a well grazed meadow, stock tanks, a small shed open on one end and a sturdy green metal gate. Water bubbled into the tank from another spring. Beyond the gate still another spring cut a small gully towards the river. The water was choked with watercress. An enormous mule deer buck watched from a bluff on the far side of the river. Ravens talked back and forth above me on bare cottonwood limbs, their large heads pointed down at me or angled to one of their companions. A few grasshoppers made half-assed attempts at leaping, tumbling into the wet grass with feeble workings of their wings. Tracks from deer covered the slate grey sandy bank along the stream. I rigged up tying on a large 2X Cree Woolly Bugger of my own design – bushy, ragged and weighted with fuse wire. Just to make sure the delicate pattern reached the bottom I pinched on an Eagle Claw butterfly shot about the size of buckshot. The tippet was 1X, a bit fine for my purposes, but I'd be gentle in my actions.

As the first cast plopped in the water along a tangle of tree trunks and limbs, the piercing "Crack" from a rifle slammed through the woods. Then silence for some seconds. Then another and another. I looked back towards the field from my now prone position in the sand through openings in the ground cover.

"Hey," I yelled as loud as possible. "Hey." No response. Was someone trying to scare me off or even shooting at me?

A white (the apparent color of choice this fall season) Cushman vehicle with a small open cab and narrow bed in back was parked directly across and 100 yards from me. Blue exhaust was riding in the now still air. I'd not heard the machine arrive in the meadow, the woods muffling the noise of its approach. Sunlight sparkled from a gun barrel but I could not see the shooter because of the leaves, wild rose bushes drooping with orange-red hips and grass. The air was thick with the lush, partially moldering smell of the

Road Fish

ground cover and I caught a whiff of the acrid cordite from the shooting. Large brown ants worked a trail through their tiny jungle a few inches from my sandy, wet face. I began to work my way in a crouch towards a spot above the cart on the edge of the field. Another shot and another.

Gunfire in the woods when I don't know where it's aimed causes an adrenalin rush comparable only to barely avoiding a head-on with a tanker truck along the Dempster Highway – shredded metal and mangled bodies scattered in the dust along the Olgilvie River. I'd hit the ground once more with feeling soaking myself in the morning dew that still dripped from everything beneath the canopy of the cottonwoods. I inched closer in my best imitation of Sargent Saunders from the sixties TV drama *Combat*. Reaching the barbed wire fence that rimmed the meadow I inched up to my knees and saw that a kid of maybe 18-19 was sighting in his rifle for the approaching big game season. He wasn't interested in me. Didn't know I was around. I relaxed, not completely, but down to Alert Level 2 from a top of 5.

I crawled under the sagging lower strand of the fence and approached the Cushman. The kid launched another round that went "Kapow." A pair of cruising mourning doves veered sharply away at the sound.

"Hello," I said.

"Hello yourself," he said slowly. Never missing a beat or seeming to notice my wet, dirty appearance he added, "I'm trying to adjust the sights on this and I'm not having any luck. Everything is high and right"

I looked off in the distance at where the Remington BDL .700 magnum (I had one identical to his) was pointing and picked out a tiny square of white against a green, brown, rust and orange background of fall color.

"How far away are we here?" I said.

"Four-hundred yards," the kid said like he'd known me all his life as I stood there holding my fly rod.

"If I were you I'd start at 200 or even 100 yards and once you're locked in at that distance, walk it back in stages to 400 if that's the distance you want. Two hundred is where I'd work from. The gun will shoot flat from there. You should be able to get that close to what your shooting at on your own land."

The kid squinted at his target, then at me. Thought on this for some time than said, "I guess you're right. I'll do that."

We than chatted on about the big game in the area, his working for his father on the ranch now that he was out of high school and the fishing in the river."

"Some of the best fishing around here is back at the creek that flows through town," he said.

I brought the rumored browns up between us and he said, "I hadn't heard about that, but go ahead and fish the river anytime you want."

He also gave me his dad's cell number adding to call before I wanted to fish just to let him know I was coming. Then he said he was heading back home to get a screwdriver, some different ammo and something to drink. He pulled down his ball cap and road off in a cloud of blue exhaust as he made his way up the coulee.

I returned to the river but the combination of rattled nerves and milky water caused by what must have been fierce storms yesterday in the mountain canyons to the south combined for a fishless outing, though I did scope out the river for future attempts next year.

~ ~ ~

The territorial bulls went silent for some reason. Two yellow-and-black Tiger Swallowtail butterflies,

Road Fish

probably the last of the year, bobbed up and down on the air as they passed over the water and disappeared through the trees. I whipped my cast towards the still-feeding brown. In my haste I missed my target by five feet to the left. A quick pick up and one more try. The fly shot out over the water and the bulls resumed roaring and stamping. The air shivered and the ground shook. The courageous Humpy landed three feet above the trout. I had overpowered the cast to beat the wind causing a left-hand curve in the leader, so no need for a mend. The bellowing increased. The righteous anger was all I could hear. I remained focused on the fly as it neared the brown that moved up and sucked the thing in with a swirl and began dropping back to its feeding spot. Lifting the rod smartly set the hook and the fish leaped then tail walked the tippet into the brush draped over the riverbank. From peripheral vision of both eyes I saw tree limbs shake, bend and shatter. At the same time the leader snapped as the brown dropped back into the water thrashing its head. Two enormous black heads and two sets of muscular shoulders crowned with humps the size of water melons, hair standing on end, now stared, stomped and screamed at each other separated by twenty-five feet of water. Apparently invisible to the two Angus, I backstopped downstream while winding in line and keeping my eyes on the bulls who continued to challenge each other for dominance of this piece of northern high plains turf.

Ginny refers to this chaos as "fishing with Holt." I guess she's correct. At least there wasn't a moose involved, but that's another sad matter for another story. By the time I'd crossed through the cottonwoods, crawled under a fence and reached the dirt road, the raging bulls' thundering was muted by distance, terrain and an afternoon wind. The mountains to the east, south and west stood silent in crystalline relief against a now cloudless sky. My sandals crunched in the stone and kicked up puffs of dust. The air smelled of the last cut of hay – sweet, herbal and dry mixing together. Looking north to where I'd just been fishing, hills marked with grey-green sage, bench land covered in native grasses turned sienna and the blue sky drifted off for miles. The pair of Tiger Swallowtails emerged from a copse of aspens and floated away ahead of me just above a rusted fence line. The craziness along the stream now seemed distant as though it never happened.

CHAPTER SEVENTEEN
Season of the Witch

When I look over my shoulder,
What do you think I see?
Some other cat looking over
His shoulder at me
And he's strange, sure is strange
                            - Donovan, *Season of the Witch*

I DISLIKE GOODBYES, saying so long to nearly anything – long ago girlfriends, the end of a trip to Canada's far north, cherished addictions – is painful like saying so long to another piece of life. The same is true for the end of fishing for the year. How many seasons are left? Was this the final one? Forcing one more day in miserable weather is not sweet agony nor does it make the ending easier. I prefer to go out in my own style. So years ago I set an arbitrary date of October 31st as the end of my fly fishing campaigns. Halloween works since some curious souls, myself included, consider this a holy day of arcane dimensions, a 24-hour period of unexpected, occasionally frightening, even twisted experience. There have been times when the rain, wind and sleet was unpleasant and there have been glorious days of light breeze, low seventies temperatures, partly cloudy blue skies framed by cottonwoods and ground cover gone berserk in autumn riparian riots of vibrant orange, gold, purple, carmine and millions of shades there in. The fishing for browns and Yellowstone cutthroat is always good in yearly variations in numbers and size, enjoyable whether casting baetis imitations, sometimes a Joe's Hopper or often the ubiquitous Woolly Bugger. The browns are adorned in intense reds, yellows, honeyed sides shading to dark backs, silvers, pure whites and grey-white lower flanks and bellies. Males with pronounced kypes (hooked and extended lower jaws) and sharp teeth often feed aggressively, an attitude mainly spawned by territorial imperative while cutthroats being cutthroats they take almost any pattern and seem to just be happy that they are included in the angling mix.

What marks this date in the past, and last year was no exception, are odd, slightly weird intrusions into my addled sense of reality that, like the fall foliage, is in other-worldly tonalities as in Merriam- Webster 's definition "the arrangement or interrelation of the tones of a work of visual art." Even the macabre, weird and out-of-kilter have their own unique artistic characteristics. I do so appreciate them. The average or serene often takes on banal appearances for me. A life of chaos and an extreme indulgence in all things altering in nature has led to this.

This was fine Halloween weather. Cool, breezy, high pewter overcast giving the day an ominous feel like someone filled with malevolent intent was watching over the fly fishing proceedings. The feel was one of winter lurking up north waiting impatiently to swoop down along the eastern slopes of the Alberta mountains and wreak frigid mayhem all over the Montana landscape. Low-grade intensity shaped the outing. It felt like something sinister was about.

A cree-hackled. brown-bodied Woolly Bugger of my own wondrous design turned brown trout heads along every brushy undercut bank, pool, moderate run or logjam in one of my favorite central Montana rivers. A slightly upstream cast and a touch of mild action and retrieve provoked swift rushes and harsh strikes followed by rapid runs for cover or downstream dashes often punctuated by several leaps with silvery spray that turned prismatic in the subdued autumn light. All of the browns ran between 14 and 18 inches. A few smaller cutthroat added to the scene. The eight-foot rod was ideal for the fishing as was the 3' JW Young reel, WF5 line, 71/2-foot leader tapered to 3x. This was a fine way to wind up the year and several more bends in the river would be enough.

Then a moose entered the play.

Because of a long-running and unsettling relationship with moose over the years – they've tracked me down and made life nervous from upper Rock Creek to Michigan's UP country to the Blackstone plateau in the Yukon – I've done a fair amount of research on the animals. In the East Siberian race of the elk the posterior division of the main fork of the moose's rack divides into three tines, with no distinct flattening. In the common elk on the other hand, this branch usually expands into a broad palmation as in the palm of the hand, with one large tine at the base, and a number of smaller snags on the free border. The palmation appears to be more marked in the North American race. The largest of all is the Alaskan race which stands eight feet in height, with a span of six feet across the antlers. Male moose weigh over 1,200 pounds on average. Only the males have antlers, averaging 63 inches across and weigh 45 pounds with a broad, flattened palmate shape fringed in up to 30 times. Although generally timid, the males become very bold during the breeding season, when the females utter a loud call, which can be heard from up to two miles away, and are often mistaken for lowing cattle; and at such times they fight both with their antlers and their hoofs. Fierce clashing of antlers between males is also not uncommon. Moose can run up to 35 mph. I can't. Moose can swim about six mph.

Road Fish

They can also submerge under the water for 30 seconds or more. These dimensions and behavioral tidbits are important where my survival is concerned. Being annihilated by a crazed beast with a prodigious appendage attached to its head has no appeal.

I remember years ago hearing of one large moose that would plant itself in the middle of the road that ran alongside the North Fork of the Flathead River every morning for a couple of weeks during the morning refusing to allow a school bus to pass. The animal would regally stand its ground with the yellow vehicle, snorting and pawing at the gravel road surface, often for more than an hour before grudgingly moving off into the timber. But for some reason the moose would move slightly aside to allow pickups and other rigs to pass. Finally things came to a head in mid-October when the moose rammed the bus repeatedly damaging the radiator which gave up the ghost in a cloud of hissing steam. The next day the angry fellow was gone and never resumed his noble antics. I've far more trouble with this species than with grizzlies. I'm always on the lookout for moose when I'm fishing and with good reason as the following will exemplify. Michael Meyers and Rob Zombie had nothing on these guys. And I do not know why they dislike me with such vehemence.

As I worked around the next turn heading for a long, deep run that was always good for a couple of big trout, loud slurping and the sound of hooves dragging across the gravel substrate rode down on the wind keeping ominous time with the burbling of the crystal current as it bounced over the streambed. Working past a stand of several dozen aspen, now full-blown and intense yellow I spotted a moose – long, ungainly legs, big rack, aquatic plants clumped in its maw dripping water and silt and malevolent, dark eyes that may have once belonged to the grim reaper.

John Holt

"Damn!" I said and the moose looked up at me. I began backing towards the aspen for shelter. They were growing close enough together that the moose would not be able to reach me because of the width its rack. This sophisticated ploy worked once before way up in the Gallatin headwaters in the early seventies when another moose came close with bad intent. This time around, I'd hold out in the trees, for days if necessary. Ten feet from shelter I looked back. The animal was coming fast, fast, fast in my direction. I bolted, all pretext of low-key retreat gone. I made the safety of this arboreal inner sanctum with no damage to the new Chris Barkley 7'9" Synthesis rod though the tippet and fly broke off on a dead goldenrod stalk. The animal was enormous and close. Maybe 15 feet, but I was protected in my natural haven. I could smell its funk and rank breath as it stalked the perimeter. Hooves sinking and making sucking sounds in the wet earth. I pulled out a cigar of decent lineage and fired it up. Fear made me trip back to yesteryear when I used to suck down Camel straights. I inadvertently inhaled and coughed out the strong smoke of the cigar. The moose stopped in its tracks and stared at me for what seemed forever. I puffed on the cigar and occupied my little pea brain thinking of famous bald people – Ken Kesey, Mick Fleetwood, Emperor Ming, Ben Kingsley. When I got to Cal Ripken and switched over to projecting what the Cubs starting rotation might be in the future – Lester, Hendricks, Quintana, Chatwood, Montgomery. This proved to be too convoluted to contemplate. I focused on the cigar taking a deep draw and expelling the thick smoke in the direction of the now motionless moose. The slightest of northeast breezes carried the acrid cloud his way and apparently up his nose. The enormous snout reared skyward, his mouth opened and emitted the loudest, wettest sneeze

Road Fish

in observed central Montana angling history. Some of the stuff blew on my face and sweater. Thoughts of an obnoxiously named beer came to mind. The moose turned and loped off towards a swampy area upstream. Crashing sounds reverberated around the narrow drainage. He never looked back or slowed. Neither did I as I hustled my way back to my '83 Suburban a couple of miles downstream.

Splashing through shallow water and along the stream edge, never far from sheltering trees, I constantly looked over my shoulder for the moose that was no longer there but was a tangible presence nonetheless. Potential mayhem made for fast progress. Just above a dark pool along a coppery colored bed of gravel I spotted a small fish struggling, writhing on its side, obviously soon to be dead. Walking closer revealed this to be a 10-inch Yellowstone cutthroat, its colors already fading as fate closed in. I watched the trout try to hold its own in the weak current when from below the edge where the stream shelved into dark water a large fish snaked up and grabbed the dying fish in its gaping jaws, the white of the inside of the mouth visible as death incarnate when it opened then clamped down. A brown of several pounds shook the cutthroat, moved its grip to the doomed fish's midsection and slunk back where it had been lurking. The last vision was of the little trout weakly fighting to free itself from that predatory grasp. Then the water was empty, lifeless. The all too real vignette made me shudder. I'll never erase that sight from my head.

The day darkened as the overcast lowered and thickened. Rain began to fall, changing to sleet then snow as a cold wind dropped in from the north. I redoubled my retreat to the sanctuary of the rig. Fishing was done for the year. The signs were clear. I'd been told.

CHAPTER EIGHTEEN
The Mining Industry Never Sleeps ...

Anarchism is founded on the observation that since few men are wise enough to rule themselves, even fewer are wise enough to rule others."
- Edward Abbey

WHAT FOLLOWS ARE A COUPLE examples of an industry that runs roughshod over the land. They never quit and will keep returning to these and other locations hoping that eventually all those who care for good country will give up or look the other way. (Since the initial writing, nothing has really changed and the mining thugs keep on keeping on.)

~ ~ ~

Smith River Drainage

I would consider the disingenuous nonsense spewed forth by the mining industry over the years laughably pathetic if the message it depicts was not so dire for Montana and elsewhere on the planet. I wrote the following paragraph July 14th 2015 in a story for Counterpunch.org about a Canadian mining company's proposal to mine gold in the upper Yellowstone near Emigrant Peak in the Paradise Valley. It held true then. More so now.

"One of the things I've learned over the decades of writing about the environment is that mining interests are determined, relentless, thorough and extremely forceful. These people won't go away. It's never too early to mount a concerted resistance to their planned malignancies. They make timber company executives

Road Fish

look like a slap-happy, costumed group of greeters at Disney World."

Enormous public pressure caused Canadian-based Lucky Minerals Inc. to back away from its planned mayhem on public lands in the Absaroka Mountains. Private holdings are another matter for now.

The latest venal insult to the natural world comes from yet another Canadian firm (they've done a fine job trashing their own country so now they look to other parts of the world – fly over Alberta and B.C. or drive up to the Cardinal coal mine near Hinton, Alberta if you don't believe me) of brief lineage calling itself Tintina Resources, Inc. It submitted its application for the Black Butte Copper Project located on private land about one mile from the Smith River tributary of Sheep Creek last Wednesday to the Montana Dept. of Environmental Quality. DEQ officials will study potential environmental effects prior to rendering a decision on whether or not to approve the application for the mine that would be about 20 miles from White Sulphur Springs.

Save Our Smith (SOS), an organization formed to stop this obscenity, describes the Smith this way, "Montana's Smith River is renowned worldwide for its clean water, rugged canyon scenery, and blue ribbon trout fishery. The Smith is Montana's only permitted recreational river. The permitted section of the Smith River winds 59 miles through a remote canyon in the Big Belt Mountains. Montana Fish, Wildlife, and Parks classifies the Smith River's fishery as high-value, owing to its bountiful population of rainbow, brown, westslope cutthroat, and brook trout. The canyon walls of the Smith also boast some of the best examples of Native American pictographs in Montana."

Tintina, headquartered in Vancouver, B.C. and

partnered with Australian-based Sandfire Resources on this project, claims the site holds one of the highest-grade copper deposits on the planet with more than 11 million tons of the ore beneath the surface.

The Smith is Montana's only permitted river due to public demand to experience its fishing and recreational opportunities. Use of the river generates more than $10 million in annual revenue from these activities. A portion of the river is managed as a State Park, featuring a 59-mile stretch of river with only one put-in and one take-out point. The Smith River and its tributaries provide crucial habitat and spawning grounds for regional trout fisheries. The Sheep Creek drainage accounts for over half of tributary spawning of rainbow trout in the Smith River drainage, and rainbow trout have been known to travel nearly 200 miles round-trip from the Missouri River to spawn.

Floating the Smith is a calming, regenerating and at times humbling experience. Floating beneath towering sandstone cliffs, camping on forested banks or catching large brown trout as abundant and varied wildlife looks on with mild curiosity is a natural process for stepping out of linear time.

According to SOS the proposed mine is particularly a concern because the copper extraction will involve digging into sulfide minerals, which when exposed to air and water, can react to form sulfuric acid in a process known as acid mine drainage. Acid mine drainage is highly toxic to fish and other aquatic life. Groundwater pumping from mining activities could potentially lower the water table, and create a "cone of depression" that extends to the Sheep Creek alluvium – posing a threat to adjacent stream flows. The Smith River and Sheep Creek suffer from low flows during most years, putting pressure on downstream water users and preventing the fishery

Road Fish

from reaching its potential. Captured groundwater will contain arsenic and other toxic substances that pose a serious threat to water quality.

One October my wife Ginny and I spent several days enjoying the Sheep Creek drainage – she photographed the land while I fished. The aspens were blazing yellow-gold. The creeks were icy clear and full of riotously colored westslope cutthroat and brook trout. Deer and elk wandered the forest while red-tailed hawks, eagles and wandering vultures cruised the thermals. At night he sky was sliced the glowing white band that is the Milky Way only slightly diminished by a rising full moon after midnight. Nighthawks boomed above us. This is a truly glorious, peaceful place. Tintina's proposed disaster would be located just a few miles from where we camped.

It is important that all of us who care for such wonders as Sheep Creek and the Smith River landscape do everything we can to stop these greedy bastards dead in their tracks and send them scurrying back home.

~ ~ ~

Emigrant Peak Gold Mine Proposal
(For now this disaster is on hold. For now ...)

The mining industry, always rapacious in its desires. Is now setting its sights on 2,500 acres in the Emigrant Peak area of the Paradise Valley, a spectacular place with rugged mountains, thick forests and cold, crystalline streams that drift down on the Yellowstone River. As usual, gold is the main quarry in this effort. Lucky Minerals Inc. (at least they didn't have the temerity to name themselves "Life Is Good Mineral Extraction Consortium"), a Surrey, British Columbia, mineral exploration company, has applied for two separate exploration permits in the area, one with the Custer Gallatin National Forest and one on private land with the Montana Department of Environmental Quality.

Emigrant Peak is the backdrop for the famous Chico Hot Springs Resort and its owner and general manager Colin Davis isn't happy about the prospect.

"It all leads to only one possibility," Davis said, "which is a massive, horrific mine back there."

Lucky Minerals, has applied for two separate exploration permits in the area, one with the Custer Gallatin National Forest and one on private land with the Montana Department of Environmental Quality. Twelve boreholes are planned for public land and 23 on private holdings to determine if further mining is financially and physically feasible. The project is in its infancy, but a coalition of environmental groups has started a campaign to try and halt the project in its tracks, seeing potential for it to lead to a massive gold mine in the Paradise Valley.

One only has to search online for photos of the Zortman goldmine in the Little Rockies near the Missouri Breaks to see what this activity leads to. A pristine Montana island mountain range has been savaged. The scars are visible from miles away. Streams that once provided habitat for native trout now run a lifeless, putrid orange. The forest surrounding the devastation is eerily quiet – few birds or mammal, large and small, live here now. And there other mines like this scattered around the state, whose motto is "oro-y-plata" – gold and silver. The Golden Sunlight mine in southwest Montana a few miles northwest of Whitehall comes to mind. Another blight that is also visible for many miles. Tainted groundwater, curious local cancer rates and the legal ability to use cyanide heap leach pit process to extract gold. The process was outlawed by Montana ballot initiative in 1998, but pre-existing operations like

Road Fish

Golden Sunlight were grandfathered in through existing or amended permits.

The Greater Yellowstone Coalition along with the Park County Environmental Council and Yellowstone Bend Citizens Council are at the forefront of the resistance. Community meetings in both Emigrant and Livingston have been held. To explore mineral deposits on a fraction of their claims, Lucky is seeking a categorical exclusion from the Forest Service and a checklist environmental assessment from DEQ. Both are lower levels of environmental analysis than other agency processes and are standard for exploration projects. The environmental groups want government agencies to give it tougher scrutiny. They say the exploration could lead to a mine three times the size of the Berkeley Pit.

If approved, drilling would have started in 2016. The plan the Forest Service was taking comments on isn't Lucky's first draft. Originally the company proposed to build some new roads for the project, but backed off of that once the Forest Service told the company it wouldn't work. Now some of the proposed drill sites are along existing roads and some are in a designated roadless area only accessible by helicopter. The DEQ part of the project is all on private land. Agency officials have visited the site and a draft of their checklist environmental assessment has been internally reviewed, but spokeswoman Kristi Ponozzo said the earliest it would be finalized is late this week.

Should the mine prove profitable, residents and visitors to the area can expect steady traffic from enormous haul trucks, degradation of air and water quality including possible serious damage to the Yellowstone's world-renowned trout fishery. Noise from the operation will be horrific, but then there is always the delightful improvement to the countryside.

Instead of enjoying a skyline of pristine, forest-covered mountains and clear streams there will be lovely scarred hillsides with a loss of habitat for elk, grizzlies and the like, degraded waters possibly devoid of fish, and merely one more piece of Montana lost to corporate greed.

Lucky has registered with the Montana Secretary of State and has a Livingston post office box, but no staff stationed in the area, sort of like the online university of Jeff Bridges' long-ago movie, Hearts of the West. That won't come until exploration is approved. A successful exploration would draw interest from large gold companies who might want to buy the claim.

"If they make us an offer we couldn't refuse, we'd take it," said Shaun Dykes, Lucky's vice president.

The process will take a few years, which is why the company thinks the outrage from the environmental groups is too early. The exploration has yet to be approved and, if it is approved, Lucky must raise $2.5 million from its shareholders to fund it. Pocket change to these boys.

All of this is strikingly familiar, reminding me of the situation in the Blackfoot River drainage near Lincoln in the western part of the state years ago. A Canadian (there all Canadian at heart in the global economy) concern planned to take down a very large hill to 1,500 feet below the valley floor while extracting gold. Fortunately in the early nineties gold prices plummeted and local resistance was fierce. And the plan is shelved, for now, although there are rumblings from the mining industry about revisiting this possibility of making this environmental disaster a dream come true.

One of the things I've learned over the decades of writing about the environment is that mining interests

Road Fish

are determined, relentless, thorough and extremely forceful. These people won't go away. It's never too early to mount a concerted resistance to their planned malignancies.

Oro-y-plata my ass.

CHAPTER NINETEEN
High Plains Autumn – Blasted on the Yellowstone

MOVING EFFORTLESSLY down the Yellowstone in early-November, mid-morning, wet snow coming down, the land all but washed away by the storm that maintains an even intensity that is not quite a blizzard. Only the dark water, rock shelves, and dormant grasslands that fade into the mist are visible, radiating slight suggestions of their true shadings like a digital color exposure converted to 80 percent black-and-white tonality.

Sounds are muted, diminished, minor echoes of themselves.

And the river flows weakly at late-season, near-drought levels, as though it's tired and needs a reprieve to rest and gather itself beneath winter's ice before regaining its raging demeanor within next spring's runoff.

None of early October's blazing exuberance remains, that flash-brief, intense period of compressed life that explodes like a supernova before days like this one arrive. Everything moves in somber rhythms that initially appear melancholy, but gradually reveal themselves as nothing more than the essence of autumn passing and working through November's moods – gray, darkening, growing colder.

~ ~ ~

Montana's northern high plains roll off forever in all directions, hundreds of miles of sage flats, coulees and bluffs filled with mystery and surprise. Maybe a small, nowhere stream is found to be full of large, eager brown trout. Or the rancher over the far ridge

Road Fish

turns out to be a great guy who makes a fantastic barbecue, even for strangers. But in all my thousands of miles of traveling across this open country only one thing out here continues to truly amaze and, at times, frighten me, and that's the weather.

The insanely unpredictable nature of the climate on the windswept prairies takes me by surprise at least several times each year. Wild, deadly electrical storms pounding the Yellowstone River east of Forsyth. Tornados in Tongue River country. One-hundred-ten degree heat on the alkali flats near Wyoming's Pumpkin Buttes. Claustrophobic fog along deadly Highway 93 in the Flathead. All of this and it never quits.

A few days ago I was driving from my home in Livingston some 330 miles north to the Sweet Grass Hills near the Canadian border. The day is stone-cold perfect autumn with temperatures in the low seventies, a soft breeze replacing the usual wicked winds. The sky is deep blue and cloudless. The October light casts the landscape with a velvet radiance that set the turning-bright-yellow cottonwoods on fire. Mountain ranges shimmer in the vibrant clarity. I have high hopes of a peaceful few nights camping next to a certain ranch pond I know, taking fat rainbows by day and reclining easily around a crackling fire at night watching countless stars come out and random meteors fizzle by overhead. No doubt coyotes will be chattering their canine jazz riffs, too.

This is not to be. Within 50 miles of the Hills a low, dark bank of clouds make an appearance, sweeping down across the Alberta line and are pushed rapidly in my direction by an Arctic air mass. When I reach the pond, the blue skies and mild temperatures are history. Icy winds are gusting over 60 miles-per-hour and driving sharp snow in my face. My laid back

October fly fishing sojourn is dead and blown away across the DRY hills towards North Dakota. The small lake is heaving with whitecaps. My old Suburban rocks side-to-side in the gale. The clouds are down near ground level swirling and boiling, seeming to explode in malevolent billowings onto the dead grasses with frigid intent.

Still, I rig up my rod and frigidly march to the water's edge. Come this far, you have to at least try. Then out of nowhere the wind dies a swift death, the pond's surface stilled to a mirror. Rainbows begin leaping and making splashy feeding rises. The cloud cover lifts to the tops of the buttes, sunlight creeps through creases in the overcast and lights up the land in a flickering cascade, sheets of sharp light washing across the native grasses like electric waves. I take trout on nearly every cast. One pound. Two. Three. The fish leap and walk on their tails across the mirrored water and through the snowflakes that vanish on the pond's surface with the small hissing sounds. This is magic, but like all magic it vanishes as quickly as it appeared. Brief instances of perfection are granted us for no apparent reason. I've learned to ride the good times for all their worth then retreat when all of it rips away south to easier temporal climates.

Within minutes the wind is roaring again, my vain attempts at casting blown away. The temperature drops to nineteen degrees. Ice begins forming along the shoreline rocks. Time to leave, beat tracks back to the railroad town of Shelby, get a warm room at the O'Hair Manor, a spicy Mexican meal at The Shelby Alamo and turn in. Maybe catch an old Sidney Greenstreet movie on some obscure cable station.

As I close the last beat-up wood and barbed wire gate behind me on the dirt road that leads to this lake, I look back to where I'd been. The buttes are gone, lost

Road Fish

in masses of dark purple spinning and boiling clouds. Snow is driving sideways from west to east and it's very cold. Not November cold. January cold.

I've been here many times before, but these first true blasts of real winter coming literally out of the blue so early in autumn while I'm so far away from everything civilized on the isolated high plains always take me by surprise. And sometimes I don't escape the action scot-free on a variety of levels as the following incident from several Novembers past might indicate.

~ ~ ~

My Suburban is stuck in the gumbo at the bottom of Bullwhacker Coulee. A storm is wailing down from the southern slopes of the Bears Paw Mountains, ice-hard snow slamming into the ground and ripping across the grey-brown countryside in a quality Montana whiteout. The light is a ghostly (ghastly?) silvery blue in the dimming light of a November afternoon. I'd been way back in this isolated bit of nowhere camping by myself for the hell of it when I saw a ragged, boiling line of spinning storm clouds beating down from the north. The weather had been crisp, autumn perfect. I'd even managed to catch a few bass in a spring-fed pond hiding out on an alkali flat. Late-night fires, Cuban cigars and what not. A peaceful time up to the point of winter's mad arrival. Throwing everything into the back of the Suburban, I thought I could beat the front if I managed to slip through this 300-foot dip in the two-track that eventually turns into a decent road, relatively speaking, that heads to Havre. A sleazy hotel room, delivered pizza, some tequila and HBO were calling. I was wrong. I didn't make it. Even creeping along in four-wheel-drive the rig begin to slip gathering speed as soon as it pointed its nose over the rise that gave way to a steep grade, but luckily slid to the bottom and then off road into the muck

John Holt

Now what? I have plenty of food, liquids and gear in the rig. Eventually this blizzard will let up, though it is howling now through the dead bunch grass and sage. Some rancher will notice the mess on his way out tomorrow or the next day. In time I'll have another foolish story to tell. The need to start a fire is obvious and there is plenty of wood in the form of gnarled limbs and sticks lying along the sides of the dry streambed and now being covered in snow.

My waxed-cotton coat and some shooting gloves are on the front seat. A wool hat is in one of the coat's pockets. Everything else I need is in the back in mildly scattered disarray. I'd attend to the tent and sleeping bag later, but first a fire and some heat. I always carry a box of Ohio Blue Tip matches in one of the coats many pockets. I clear a spot in the snow in the lee of a boulder, lay in a pile of twigs and sticks. I'm beginning to ease off the adrenalin rush of the motorized mayhem. The thought of freezing to death out here flashes briefly then slips away with the swirling wind. I begin to think of family and friends as I prepare to strike the first match.

The flame is bright in the gloom and I imagine that I see my mother sitting in front of the fireplace at her home in Whitefish sipping her customary evening Old Fashion. She turns to me in the flickering light of the match and says, "I always told you to get a cell phone. You never know when something like this will happen and now it has. I hope you weren't drinking when this happened." I hadn't been, though based on past exploits this was a reasonable inquiry. Mom has always been on my side, right there with me through all of the chaos I manage to stagger into, but I find it odd that all of this was taking place within the bright confines of a match flame flickering in my cupped hands. "Call me when you get home," and she turns to

Road Fish

the fire, sips her drink and the match goes out.

I find a couple of yellow receipts from Napa Auto Parts in my pocket – brake pads and a headlight – and work them beneath the twigs. I strike a Blue Tip and it fizzles, smokes and dies. I rip another along the side of the box and it catches. Shoving it next to the paper, hunching over to protect it with my body, the beginnings of fire curls up to the wood. In the light this time I see a woman I'd known briefly some years ago. I think to myself 'Holt, you're truly nuts this time around.' But there she is, well-tanned, short brown hair, sitting in a chaise lounge on the front porch of her home along the Bitterroot. I can see the thick green grass of her front yard, the crabapple trees and across the gravel road a farmer working a hayfield in the last of the day's sunlight. Her name is Shannon and she says quite clearly, her voice sounding like there is no storm raging around me at all, "You know John, if you weren't such an outspoken loner you'd have more friends. As it is now, you either scare the hell out of us or piss us off with your hardcore pronouncements. Ease up on us, would you? And do yourself a favor and cut yourself some slack," and she lights a cigarette with a silver lighter before concluding with "Just go away for good and leave us in peace," and Shannon draws on her smoke before blowing out a thick blue cloud of smoke. A puff of iced wind snuffs out the match and the paper.

Nuts or not, I don't need this. I need a fire and then a few drinks. I get up, already stiff from the cold and the lovely weather, lurch over to the Suburban for a can of lighter fluid. I like to cheat at times. I return to my pile of sticks that is somewhat sheltered by the boulder dropped off in this location thousands of years ago by a friendly glacier. The wood gets doused with fossil fuel, then I pull the box of matches from my coat and try again. Man, just give me some serious flame and none of this concerned advice silliness, though I am curious to see who will show up next.

The match sizzles and bursts into flame, the fuel ignites easily and the small sticks began to pop and crackle. I'm home or rather, because of the madness of the wavering flames, I'm sitting on the front steps of my old friend Bob Jones' home. He is rubbing the ears of his yellow lab Jake. He turns to me and starts to say something...

"Don't interrupt me, damnit," he said. "We've been friends for a long time. Been through hell and back more than once," and he reaches down for a stick that he tosses in some tall grass. Jake leaps to the chase. "You always run along the precipice of things looking for trouble. Your life isn't some twisted Nabokov novel like *Ada* or *Laughter in the Dark*. And it sure as hell isn't *Lolita*. Ease up on yourself. Relax a little. I'd suggest finding a good woman, but we both know how that would turn out. So, get the damn fire going and don't pay any attention to what Shannon just said. Make yourself a stiff drink and ride out the night. We've got those browns on the Marias to play with next year." I start to say something, but a wicked downdraft of frigid air packed with snow mashes my fire into nothing. I smell damp smoke.

Even while I am courting hypothermia, I realize that I am having an episode of sorts. One that is odd even in my arcane experiences. Perhaps I really am nuts or, at least, making a game effort to go in that direction.

"Screw it," I say and return to getting the fire going.

I pour a fair amount of lighter fluid and strike a lot of matches, and also hear from a lot of people during the next thirty minutes, but the gods eventually take

Road Fish

pity on me and the wood finally burns. I build the sucker up into a blaze by diligently adding stick upon larger stick. Maybe the muddy landing on the road up above has driven me crazier than normal. Maybe I am having a brief interlude with mortality. Whatever. In the coals that glow in the darkness of early night I see everything that is the West for me —my friends, the freedom of isolation and the peaceful side of the wide-open lonesome land. I begin to warm up and think of getting some more wood and making at least the illusion of shelter. The whiteout has transmogrified into a straightforward snowfall. The wind is all but dead and large flakes drift down, many of them turning to vapor above fire.

I'd decide that I've had enough conversation for one evening. I walk over to the Suburban, my boots pushing through a half-foot of snow, in search of a bottle of whiskey to build that stiff drink Bob suggested.

CHAPTER TWENTY
A Little Traveling Music

HOW IN THE HELL did I get here? I've fished this stretch of the Shields River many times, but everything seems madly changed in the most unnoticeable of ways. I've been here spring, summer and, finest of all, autumn.

Early October is when large browns lose their secretive, shadowy behavior. The trout, now driven by the spawning urge, are roaming the shallow, gravel runs where the females will build their redds in earnest in a week or so. In summer they are holding-out way back in the darkness of brushy, undercut banks. Most times browns are secretive, loners. Even the chaotic splash of a suicidal grasshopper a few feet out in the open water rarely causes them to move. Nymphs, minnows, smaller trout, any of these that happen to wander in front of the large predators will be killed quickly, but otherwise they won't budge. I know. I've tried launching everything from woolly buggers to hefty nymphs to saltwater patterns like Deceivers a few feet out from the bank to try and provoke movement. Rarely will one of the browns take my offering, one made with the most honest of intentions. I want to connect, to feel a wild fish as it runs for cover at the bite of the hook or walks and crashes along the surface. The trout's fight for survival makes me feel alive. Perhaps a cruel way to get one's kicks, but I'm a predator, too – an emotional one above all else.

So after taking a half-dozen browns, a small brook trout and a Yellowstone cutthroat, everything is pretty much as I've always remembered it over the years. I notice this as I sit down on a fallen tree trunk along the

Road Fish

bank. The stream is low and clear. The streambed sparkles in gem-like colors beneath the gold-copper light of the fall sun. The leaves on willows, birch and cottonwoods are going brilliant yellow, manipulating light in carefree ways. The undergrowth is a mixture of colorful life and death – the buff browns of dying grasses swirled with riffs of crimson and purple from wild berries and rosehips. The freshly white peaks of the Crazies are visible over the ridge in the east and the Bridgers glow dark-blue, grey and white to the west. Shadows tinted in the same shades creep down the mountain cirques and valleys as the sun moves west. A pair of sandhill cranes clacks away in that dying grass. I see their heads and necks bobbing and lurching as they strut away from me. Strings of geese are moving south with their common cries. Pairs of mallards whistle through the air. Deer silently observe my movements from a distance, as do Angus cattle that pause from their loud munchings to check me out. The last dregs of this year's mayflies bounce above the river's surface. Ahead I see an oval depression of newly cleared stone. The first brown trout spawning bed. One of many that will be dotted along this isolated stretch of water before much longer.

Yeah, all of this seems the same, but just like the end of last season and the one before and so on, everything is different in ways that are visible, but not to the eyes. This valley and everywhere else I travel in Montana at this time of the year seems to have shifted to a slightly different slice of time than the one I'm buzzing in. There's just enough of this movement to make me feel as though I'm in the middle of the gentlest of earthquakes or passing through a mild moment of dizziness. I feel like I'm in a room where the furniture has been subtly rearranged with such sophistication that I don't notice the changes.

John Holt

I know I'm crazy. Have been so as long as I can remember. I once had some concern about this to the extent that I used to down large quantities of whiskey to try and feel sane. Didn't work. Drunk is drunk, and hungover is hell growing ever larger as I got older. The changes I'm experiencing aren't associated with being loony. They seem to be more involved with experience and the smallest of advancements in awareness. One would think that an individual as self-absorbed as myself would see any growth in perception as enormous, but it doesn't work that way. And I've noticed all of this for years in a number of places. Fishing's to blame. Hanging out in undisturbed nowhere is at fault. Casting to trout or bass or pike is strong stuff, much stronger than the whiskey I mentioned. The power has little to do with landing a large trout, though, like sex, following fly fishing to its commonly accepted conclusion is of brief satisfaction.

I first drifted through this mild oddity in vision a dozen years ago down in Tongue River country, the home of my heart. The coulees, eroding rock, native grasses, turkeys, coyotes and the vast aloneness are sensible to me. One October I'd shot a pair of sharptail grouse on a flat just off the red-dust two-track that winds to a dry camp I have near a stand of old Ponderosa. There were lots of the birds feeding on fat crickets. When they took wing at my approach, their flight was labored. The shooting straightforward. Next I drove to a pond that used to hold rainbows, still does in a non-fishing way. An hour of relaxed casting netted me several trout. I killed one to go with my grouse-baked potato-roasted onion dinner. As I was cleaning this fish I felt as though the landscape slipped sideways. I put the rainbow in the cooler on ice, opened a Pabst, lit a smoke and looked around. The land was silent. Nothing but yellow sunlight shifting

Road Fish

towards orange moving over the country dragging purple shadows with it. This was as alone as I'd ever felt. Like the only person on the planet. In some ways I was terrified. Then giving in to the unnamed but obviously deep fear, a sense of power ripped through me. The rush faded. I have no concept of what is meant by serenity, but I felt at peace for the first time in I don't know how many damn years. What had I done to earn this respite from the day-to-day anxiety? Well, I'd walked a windy flat, killed a couple of birds and then fished for some trout. Nothing more or less. Not one for examining my psychological navel, I finished my beer and moved on.

Since that little country ditty there have been many other moments of oh-so-modest revelation. Fishing the Yellowstone here in Livingston with a longtime friend. Hooking a brown and then slipping on a rock, falling in and gaily floating downstream with the angry fish pulling on my line as I tried to keep the rod above water and avoid drowning. I lost the fish, but saved my life. I remember the sound of my companion laughing from his vantage point on a high cut bank and his yelling "Holt, I can't understand why Orvis won't send you any more stuff. You're fly fishing's poster child." And then that slight lateral shift of reality, life, whatever, materialized. A touch of fear, aloneness (not loneliness, that's something else) and then happy calm. I doubt I would have felt this way at a sports bar or a concert or a restaurant.

I've never been much for fishing with guides or doing the in thing like traveling to the latest hot river or lodge or far off country. I'm a true loner, like the browns, and simpler is better. It avoids confusion and eventual torment. This is how fly fishing, bird hunting, any outdoor avocation, was shown me. Catching fish – yes, that's nice. Killing a few pheasants – not bad either. Owning quality gear that makes all of this easier and more enjoyable – nothing wrong here. But that's not really the point. Those who have patiently guided me along a life that centers on good country have all said in their own curious ways, "That's cool that you made that cast that caught that fish, but that's not what's important. What counts, kid, is that river you're standing in. Those mountains over there. That blood-red prairie we crossed at sunrise – how all of it makes you feel. That's the game you're really after."

And I finally grasped the natural concept. Basically it's brain-dead simple. Lose the ego. Submit to the land. Connect with the feral buzz, then recognize my insignificant yet worthwhile place in the untamed, unfathomable scheme of things. None of the good stuff is related to fancy clothing, pricey fly rods or $5,000-a-week lodge gigs. Get wet and a little muddy. Then feel good enough to slide along in a strange dance for no good reason.

The light of October is special. It glows with an amber influence. I look up from my tree-trunk seat and spot a brown holding in a soft run about forty feet upstream. Only its fins and slight flicks of its tail reveal motion. Slowly I work out line to cover the distance, make the cast and start the retrieve. The fish hits the pattern with its head once, then again. It circles back and slams the streamer. The white of its mouth flashes. This fish thrashes across the surface, tires quickly and comes easily to me as I kneel in a few inches of water. Reds, browns, blacks, pale greens and bronze flanks. The lower jaw is formed into a hook or a kype. A male. I twist the hook free and watch as the trout swims slowly across stream to a deep hole beneath the tangled roots of an old cottonwood. And my fragile, lunatic world shifts casually out of kilter. I'm a bit afraid, then serene again, then laughing. "Completely nuts, Holt," I say out loud to no one; and feel good about it all.

CHAPTER TWENTY-ONE
Montana Stream Access –
Trout Rustling Gone Mad

GREED, INSECURITY AND JUST PLAIN OLD "I got mine, screw you" bullshit is making itself more and more apparent in Montana when it comes to fly fishing (and many other things). The situation often involves big-money yahoos locking up land access to prime waters by purchasing leases from ranchers who own acreage on one of both sides of rivers flowing through their property. These leases effectively close off access to trout streams or make reaching the waters an extremely difficult and lengthy process. Former network news readers, has-been movie stars, over-the-hill writers and yuppie arbitragers are all part of a concerted effort by a few to deny fly fishing to many – a tangible metaphor for the escalating land grab perpetuated by the terminally wealthy not only in Montana but much of the West.

Aside from the fact that the state has some of the finest trout waters anywhere in the world – the Madison, Yellowstone, Bitterroot, Bighorn, Beaverhead and on and on, what sets the state apart from the rest of the country and also the world is its stream access law that gives anglers the right to fish on nearly every river, stream and creek that flows out here.

Montana is unique among other Western states and most states in general. In 1984, the Montana Supreme Court held that any river or stream that has the capability to be used for recreation, such as fishing and floating, can be used by the public regardless of whether or not the river is navigable and who the

Road Fish

owner of the streambed property is. The result is that anglers and floaters have full use of most of the rivers in Montana for fishing and floating, along with swimming and other river related activities. This is known as the Montana Stream Access Law, a law that has been under attack by out-of-state interests since its inception.

On Mitchell Slough in the Bitterroot Valley, a stream local residents have fished for decades, wealthy out-of-staters attempted to close access but were overruled when the Montana Supreme Court ruled in 2008 that the 16-mile-long stream is open to the public and that the landowners are not entitled to fence it off as part of their private sanctuaries. The court said the slough roughly follows the historical course of a waterway mapped 130 years ago, and therefore is subject to public access and required permitting, as are other natural waterways. The 54-page decision overturned two earlier rulings by state district courts that found the slough was not a natural, perennial-flowing stream.

Opponents to the law as it applied to the slough include former pop star Huey Lewis, Charles Schwab, Private Wealth Partners managing director Kenneth Siebel and a home belonging to Anthony Marnell II, the head of a casino construction company, is built over a tributary to Mitchell Slough.

In 2006 Lewis said in The Times that those in favor of public access on Mitchell Slough had "done a masterful job of casting this as a class-warfare issue... 'Rich out-of-staters' is an expletive, and they try to make it a battle against them and rich out-of-staters," he said. "There are 25 people, and 20 are not rich and not out of state." Lewis also said of Montana that there is "more cheese, fewer rats" than in California.

Montana's law was passed in response to a 1984

state Supreme Court ruling that granted public access to all surface waters "capable of recreational use," regardless of who owns the streambed, because surface waters are state property, held in public trust. The stream-access law narrowed that ruling, allowing recreational access to all "natural water bodies" but exempting private irrigation ditches. The law was challenged in 1987, and the court confirmed its intent.

In 2011, Rep. Jeffrey Welborn, a Republican from Dillon, tried another tack to curb the Stream Access Law: clarifying its prohibition on recreational access to ditches. The bill sought to broaden the definition of a private ditch to include many public waterways. It would have prevented anglers and floaters from using all waterways where the return flows from irrigation make up the majority of the flow, as well as side-channels of braided rivers and streams where irrigation controls are located at the head of the braid.

Critics say the bill was extreme, not only reversing the Mitchell Slough decision, but also seriously restricting Montanans' stream-access rights. Under it, even the Bitterroot River would be defined as a ditch, according to Bob Lane, a chief legal counsel for Montana Fish, Wildlife and Parks, because of the amount of water diverted from it during irrigation season.

"In fact, almost all rivers and streams in Montana, except those in wilderness areas and the headwaters of streams on Forest Service land, could no longer be used by the public," Lane said in a High Country News article last year. "(The bill) not only doesn't work, it just doesn't make any sense."

Former Montana U.S. Attorney Bill Mercer, a paid shill for the proposed legislation, says it simply aimed to restore the original purpose of the 1985 Stream Access Law, which was, he says, to preclude recreational use of water after it leaves the main body for irrigation. The bill won approval in the House, but died in the Senate Agriculture, Livestock and Irrigation Committee.

Bitterroot Valley fat cats are primary backers of the elitist legislation, but singer Huey Lewis claims "It ruined the Mitchell. The idea of that becoming a good fishery is over. It was becoming a spawning area -- kind of a nursery -- for the Bitterroot River, that's gone. ... It's going to become the mud ditch it was when we first found it."

Good old has-been Huey may be right, though I doubt it. If he is, he can always go back to Pebble Beach and play golf with his corporate buddies.

And individuals and guiding operations are just as greedy as private landowners. Leases are being bought up to exclude the common man from fishing streams like Sixteen Mile, the Shields and on and on. Someone I once thought of as a friend has tried (he seems to think quite subtly) to discourage me from fishing a stretch of the Shields. I little bit of investigating turned up that he was leasing access in the area from a rancher notorious for his narrow-mindedness. Such is life. I'll fish this stretch whenever I damn please.

Along the North Fork of the Blackfoot River a large fly-fishing outfitter/guiding operation has run fence directly up to a bridge (public land) crossing the stream in violation of the law. This practice is common throughout the state. On a recent trip I noticed this exclusionary practice on bridges spanning streams that included the Dearborn, the Musselshell drainage, Swift Creek, the Yaak drainage and the Teton.

No big deal you say. There's plenty of public access through state holdings, national forests, BLM and national parks. Perhaps, but should the state's access law ever be overturned, and it's under threat every second of its life, kiss goodbye fishing to a lot of rivers like those mentioned above along with others that include the Ruby, Boulder, Big Spring Creek, Blackfoot and on down the line. Large portions of these rivers wander through private holdings.

In April 2009 Montana's governor Brian Schweitzer signed HB190 – the stream access bill that allows landowners to build fences that keep cattle in, but not those that keep fly fishermen out. This is an important victory against out-of-state landowners and developers who have spent loads of cash from a large war chest in a greedy attempt to overturn the access law.

Anglers in the state may fish between the ordinary high water marks of a stream. The Montana legislature in 1985 defined the ordinary high water mark as: "Ordinary high-water mark" means the line that water impresses on land by covering it for sufficient periods to cause physical characteristics that distinguish the area below the line from the area above it. Characteristics of the area below the line include, when appropriate, but are not limited to deprivation of the soil of substantially all terrestrial vegetation and destruction of its agricultural vegetative value. A flood plain adjacent to surface waters is not considered to lie within the surface waters' high-water marks.

This means that an angler or a floater has full recreational use of a river below the rivers ordinary high-water mark. Recreational use is considered to be:

"Recreational use" means with respect to surface waters: fishing, hunting, swimming, floating in small craft or other flotation devices, boating in motorized craft unless otherwise prohibited or regulated by law,

Road Fish

or craft propelled by oar or paddle, other water-related pleasure activities, and related unavoidable or incidental uses.

A fly fisher can fish and float with non-motorized craft with only a handful of specific restrictions that are listed in the most recent fishing regulations. Motorized watercraft have further restrictions on their use (these restrictions are there to prevent conflicts between motorized boats and floaters / wade anglers / float anglers).

Since the Montana stream access law applies to virtually all rivers and streams in Montana that are found on private property, many of these rivers are quite small and have various man-made and natural obstructions in the river. A floater or angler who encounters these obstructions may also climb above the high water mark to get around these obstructions in the least intrusive way possible. The statute clearly states that this is legal; but the law does not give the public right to cross private property to reach the rivers.

Obviously wealthy landowners who thought that they were buying their own private Montana are angry. The conflict comes because the Montana Stream Access Law says the public owns the rivers. For recreation, including hunting and fishing, everyone has a right to get access to virtually any waterway that flows through private land. But many landowners have put up fences to keep people away from the streams, an act that is now in violation of the Stream Access Law.

For example, lack of access to the Ruby River has discouraged anglers. There have been a number of complaints from fishermen who have been yelled at and photographed and who have even heard warning shots fired as they fished prized trout streams flowing through private land, which is legal as long as they stay within the high-water marks.

The fight is contentious to say the least along the Ruby River, designer trout water with a good population of large brown trout that hold tight to brushy banks and along the bottoms of sapphire runs and pools. The river drifts through a valley of landowners who have put up fences to keep people off most of the river's lower stretch.

Some landowners "erroneously are trying to lay claim to a public resource," said Dick Oswald during the height of the conflict a few years ago. Oswald is a fisheries biologist for the Montana Department of Fish, Wildlife and Parks in nearby Dillon. "I suspect they didn't do their homework before they bought land. This is America, not feudal Europe."

"Montana has the last of the wild trout fisheries; the rest are shot," said Reid Rosenthal in an article in the New York Times in 1997, president of Country Roads, a company in Sheridan that manages many ranches that have been bought by wealthy fishermen and sells fishing vacations along the Ruby River. His view is typical of those opposed to the stream access law.

Rosenthal said he and his clients did not oppose public access to the Ruby but wanted a change in regulations that allow each angler to keep five trout a day. Mr. Rosenthal said allowing such catches would destroy the fishery. But proponents of public access point to a memorandum Rosenthal wrote to his ranch-owning clients in support of fund-raising for a campaign to overturn the Stream Access Law by taking it to Federal District Court, and the Supreme Court, if necessary. In the memorandum, made public by the pro-access Montana Wildlife Federation, Mr.

Road Fish

Rosenthal said, "Don't kid yourself, this situation is really one of social resentment, jealousy and envy, not fishing access."

Perhaps tired of all of the flack he received for his elitist position Rosenthal later said that he no longer supported a campaign to repeal the access law. "I wish I'd never written that damned thing."

Former Montana governor Brian Schweitzer has said the state is committed to defending the river access law. "If you want to buy a big ranch and you want to have a river and you want privacy, don't buy in Montana. The rivers belong to the people of Montana." So far, to his credit, Schweitzer has not backed off this statement.

For now people can access Montana's trout streams even if they have to climb over, under or go around obstructions like those presented by the outfitter on the Blackfoot. But everywhere I go I hear stories (hopefully just that, stories) of out-of-state Montana landowners building up a huge war chest to wage yet another attack on Montana's Stream Access Law. Whitefish poster boy, Secretary of the Interior Ryan Zinke currently represents everything that is obnoxious both in the stream access fight and in Whitefish, a once gorgeous small town I used to call home now turned into a self-absorbed hell hole.

"The attempt to make heaven on earth invariably produces hell," said Austrian philosopher Karl Popper; and Jefferson said, "The price of freedom is eternal vigilance."

Concerning the state of trout fishing and public land use in Montana and the West, nothing could be more applicable than those two comments.

CHAPTER TWENTY-TWO
Autumn Distillate

A BASIC BENCH OF ELONGATE, north-south dimensions offers vistas of unimagined elegance. Aging, rounded mountains marked by spare copses and wavering bands of weathered Ponderosa hold the northern sky. Native grasslands, dry alkali lake beds, deep green ponds filled with spring-fed, sweet water and ringed with dying cattails, desiccate coulees choked with Russian thistle, and eroding bluffs that look like paws of immense panthers drift away in the other three compass directions. Farther off, east, the Little Rockies shine golden orange in the softening light of late afternoon. Several antelope work easily along the side of a brown swale a mile down from this place, black-masked faces working alertly up and down as their white rumps tag along. Fifty yards away mule deer noisily paw at the ground searching for moist Blue grama roots through a mat of dead grass, wind-blown pine needles, cones and white-grey dust. A soft breeze rises up the far side of this rise in a forgotten moan, wanders across the flat carrying the remains of summer's heat, then blows up above me in a quick push that dies out below small tufts of cloud that thin perceptibly from the event. This hemisphere is gradually turning its back on the sun for now. The star appears to have shifted down south – merely a case of human erratic perception and arrogance waging its futile battle with the constancy of its life source. A subconscious attempt to control what is little understood, feared. This light's angle of incidence is flatter, now slanting through the air as a mixture of amber, gold, yellow and crimson. Looking at the landscape is like seeing the world through a crystal tumbler of the finest bourbon gentled slightly with spring water, perhaps from nearby ponds. None of the other days in the year compare to these finely-tuned wonders of late September and early October, not the bright green burstings of spring or the hot gems of summer or the soft white mysteries of deep winter. There is a perfection here, an essence distilled to intense yet subtle radiance that always makes me wonder if I'm still traveling across the same planet I now barely recall from just a couple of months past – late July and its parched heat mixed with wildfire smoke. Was that part of this world? Was it real?

Next-day-waking on this bench, tarp-pad-sleeping bag for a bed, as the sun rises above the distance of the Little Rockies, the eastern horizon goes from black to silver to variations of reds and orange before the skyline blazes in light too intense to quantify with colorful names. The brilliance temporarily silences mourning doves calling to each other from nearby trees. Even a raucous trio of ravens cuts its jive. The intense display causes an opposite effect among the cattails down below as dozens of red-winged blackbirds fire salvos of their wildly electric calls back and forth. Crimson wing bands that are this species' hallmark glow in the new day's radiance. Indigo shadows cast by mountains and bluffs that at first stretched, undulated for hundreds of yards across the rough prairie, visibly withdraw looking like phantasmic arms during the sun's ascension, as though they are being drawn back into that distant nuclear source that now dominates everything out here. Frost that cast prismatic reflections during first light turns to clear droplets hanging from the seed tops of the sere grass, crystalline rainbow colors flash miniature magic in the air. This moisture soon becomes faint steam. Then it's gone, the land dry once again.

The day warms, moves along. Coffee, orange juice, a couple of dry bagels before packing water, sourdough, cheese, summer sausage, apples, shotgun shells – 20-gauge, larger fly patterns like buggers, Sheep Creeks, miniscule dries of no name and personal design, extra tippet, grabbing the Berretta over-under in the oiled sheepskin and canvas case slung over shoulder, a one-ounce-two-weight in black tube doubling as walking stick, then side hilling and sliding down the grassy slope to the ponds scattered like favored emeralds across the pink, ochre, slate, purple of the exposed flats and eroding faces of the hills. Several miles away a wall of buff-colored sandstone winds around the top of a rocky dome looking like the ramparts of a castle long abandoned by those who once valued isolation and remote purity. Hundreds of feet below this are many acres of green watered by a buckled-pipe sprinkling system that shoots spray and sporadic gouts of water across domesticated grass. Timothy? Alfalfa? Whoever is doing this is out of sight, vanished. The only signs of habitation are a crumbling assemblage of homestead buildings – brown-to-grey wood frame home, log out buildings – and a few pieces of rusting machinery that was new a century ago. Scanning through binoculars, gnarled crabapple trees show their beaten trunks rising above cracked soil, the small fruit deep orange marked with charcoal imperfections.

Passing along the first pond, electric blue damselflies zip through the cattails or hover inches above the glassy surface of dark water. The brief morning breeze, cool but holding seams of the mid-day warmth to come, is gone. The air is still. Small mayflies rise crazily into the air along the edges of a

Road Fish

spring that bubbles a few feet from shore. Small fish splash after them. The dark shapes of smallmouth bass, large fish, no doubt planted by the invisible rancher, cruise the edges of the cattails feeding on the damsel and mayfly nymphs/larvae and the smaller fish, the white of their open mouths visible as they slash at angles when feeding. There will be time to take a couple of these on the return back up the rise to the bench. That's later. In another time.

Several hundred yards beyond all of this the ground appears parched, crusted with off-white salts. Stepping onto this, my boots sink into clinging jet-black mud caused by an invisible seep turning a twenty-foot crossing into an effort. On the far side is a trail of prints, four-toed, wide pad, the track of a large cat, pressed inches into the moist earth. They lead to the mountains, eventually disappearing amid the clumps of bunch grass that grow, barely, in the baked, rocky dirt. A discarded skin from a milk snake is impaled on prickly pear spines, the membrane shriveled from exposure, the formerly vibrant bands of red, black and white now lifeless, opaque parodies of the real thing. The animal must have used this open place to shed its scaly covering before sliding off to hide beneath a rotting log nearby while its new skin hardened. Glassing the hills shows a band of elk working up towards a pocket of trees in a small crease that probably holds some water.

Looking to the northwest the sky holds so blue it approaches black. An hour of this walking, often punctuated with the strong aroma of crushed juniper branches that block the way, creates a rhythm that is natural, appropriate to this day and this landscape. With temperatures climbing to seventy, soon higher, the last of this season's grasshoppers spring into action, making lengthy, clacking leaps from grass stem to bare rock to sage brush. A pair of Western meadowlarks dives bush-top level snaring some of the slower, smaller insects. The black-and-white of a skunk is visible as the animal abandons its normal nighttime routine this time of year to root among stones and moss surrounding the moistness of an ephemeral spring. I angle away from the busy thing aiming for a cut in the cliffs that leads to a creek holding tiny brook trout. Sharp-tailed grouse always hold beneath the flattened stands of juniper that grow on either slope. The trout are too small to eat, but the brookies' colors glow at this spawning time in their lives. A grouse or two, a couple of the bass, a little bourbon around a reasonable fire, a cigar. A casual touch down to end the day. Sitting on a slab of sandstone that broke away from the cliff above centuries ago, I eat some sausage, cheese, fruit, drink a little water. A mile or two to go. The grouse kick up at my approach and I mark where they land for the return in a few hours. (The word "I" is used in this, but there is no longer any pretense regarding identity or the self-important "I." When far out this way coasting solitaire, nothing matters any more. A bothersome, self-absorbed ego is shed like the snake did with its skin. "I" is merely narrative artifice here.)

An artifice of little value beneath this sun with no one to see me.

Perhaps and anon, I chatter to the voice as I often do these days, talking out loud becoming a high art as my time passes. Then play on, I mutter, play on to the tiny fish and later some dead birds for dinner, then to the shadowed soarings of several dozen gregarious Swainson's Hawks winging their way to winter in South America. A rare sight, indeed. Quite strange, but then as they say ... when you're a stranger ... and while we're at it, who the hell needs whiskey these days and

Road Fish

a chorus of plaintive *krees* issue from the soaring *Buteo* migration.

Kree it is then. Continue on Holt. You're mad as a hatter and growing much better at this latest illusion.

As it should be and thoughts of not-needed whiskey consumed around tonight's essential fire run circle round my head. We, my voices and I, continue on through the gap leading to the brook trout while groups of sharptails break from dense cover at our approach in a lunatic cacophony of guttural clucks, cackles and frantically beating wings. Mad as I can be and happily drifting through this intense fall paradise that I've yet to fall from, graceful or otherwise.

Hours later and the day's gone dark, but the sky is riddled with stars that have dropped down to ground level, surrounding me in a special silver glow that is further heightened by the ghosting green of the northern lights. The tiny brook trout that I caught on #24 dries, fish the size of my index finger, linger in my vision like brightly-colored, high-caliber bullets of blood red, cerulean, white, black, orange and on and on. These hues matching the explosion of colorings that ripped from the ground, the sage, the bluffs, the coulees, the sky when the sun touched the western horizon not all that long ago. That's when coyotes all around me launched insanely happy choruses of barking, howling and syncopated sounds I'd never heard before, continuing on with the jazz-like madness until a crescent moon made an appearance. The animals stilled, their talk replaced by the boomings of night owls working the air for bugs. I climbed the rise to camp tired and truly at peace, an uncommon deal when back in town.

The grouse are split in half, lightly seasoned and roasting on a grill over a modest bed of coals. The bass were finished first, fried in butter and peanut oil with a little sea salt and freshly ground black pepper. A few handfuls of grapes, too. I've had one whiskey and plan to have several more, and that cigar I mentioned, as I sit on the ground next to the fire.

Looking around and above me at all of this, feeling the air cool, recalling all I've experienced in one short, but eternal day I revel in the terror that is the recognition of the absolute aloneness of living this eternal existence. Concentrated days of beauty, a little truth, but not too much, that's what autumn is for me.

CHAPTER TWENTY-THREE
Wyoming Cutt-Slam – Close But No Cigar

FOR SOME OF US not making the uncommon effort to define failure and success on our own terms can transform life into a largely a disappointing experience. For example, I interpret the hundreds of book and magazine proposals that have been blithely rejected by uncaring, jaded editors and publishers over the years as nothing more than the inability of near moronic individuals to recognize wit and brilliance on my part. Losing my hair is perceived as a sign of high testosterone levels. And on it goes through convoluted time.

So when Ginny and I set out for the hinterlands of western Wyoming in search of what the Wyoming Game and Fish Department calls the Wyoming-Cutt Slam I had already internally acknowledged that I would probably not catch (and release) the four sub-species of cutthroat trout in question – Yellowstone (*Oncorhynchus clarki bouvieri*), Bonneville (*Oncorhynchus clarki utah*), Colorado (*Oncorhynchus clarki pleuriticus*) and Snake River (proposed classification of *Oncorhynchus clarki behnkei*). If I do succeed I will need to submit a form stating where and when I caught the individual cutthroat along with digital photo documentation of each variety. Then I will receive a color certificate honoring my achievement. There are no expectations on my part concerning fulfilling the Slam, but should this eventuate, I definitely plan on having the full-color certificate framed and hung in a prominent location in one of our bathrooms.

Road Fish

I'm not into competition or quest of any kind. I was initially reluctant to participate in the program, but reading the information on the department's website changed my mind. It stated that the Cutt-Slam is "A program designed to encourage anglers to learn more about Wyoming's cutthroat sub-species and develop more appreciation and support of the Wyoming Game and Fish Department's cutthroat management program." I much prefer native species to introduced gamefish as in casting to the Westslope and Yellowstone cutthroat, mountain whitefish, Montana arctic grayling (*Thymallus arcticus montanus*) and Bull trout as opposed to what most fly fishers prefer chasing – brook, brown and rainbow trout.

Inured to what most psychologically healthy individuals term abject failure, I figured two, possibly three, species landed would be a rousing success, but I had little idea how this peripatetic angling road trip would play out. The slowly realized sinister nature of the adventure will haunt me for the remainder of my life, maybe even threatening the long-term stability of my rock-solid marriage.

As I was once again to experience, the angling gods are a capricious and cruel lot.

We set out for the South Fork of the Shoshone River outside of Cody near the southeastern corner of Yellowstone Park. The road was paved degenerating into gravel winding through development after development then a long-running series of trophy and dude ranches. Once on the Shoshone National Forest every trailhead and turnout was jammed with pickups and SUVs pulling horse trailers. The high country big game season was in full swing. Despite all of this human degradation, the sharp, jagged mountain peaks, escarpments and sawtooth ridges are spectacular especially with a fresh dusting of pure white snow. At the end of the road we stop and work our way up a trail to some passable pocket water. There are excellent pool and riffle stretches all along the way to the parking spot but all of this water is on private land and therefore off limits. This is unlike Montana where an angler can access water from public roads and bridges and wade to his heart's content as long as he stays within the high water marks, in Wyoming water that flows through private holdings is PRIVATE! No exceptions. We tend to take this freedom for granted in Montana, but it is truly a gift not to be squandered or given up to out-of-state wealthy who have accumulated a massive war chest in an attempt to overturn the state's stream access law. Not on my watch. Not while I'm still kicking.

On this trip I packed a number of specialty rods that I don't use all that much but treasure nonetheless. For the South Fork I rigged up an Orvis 6-0', one-ounce, two-weight – a deceptively strong and accurate rod. Lightweight rods are a delight on small streams such as this one as long as the fish are played quickly so that they are not exhausted to the point of dying. Attached to the end of a 4x tippet is a Royal Wullf. The first four casts to likely looking holes produce small Yellowstone cutts that run in splashing circles briefly then came splashing to my wet hands. Ginny photographs the little guys as I admire them and before turning them free.

The South Fork is far too residential and locked up for our wild tastes so we decide to cut the fishing short and move on down the roads. Since we have a long distance to cover for our next cutthroat adventure somewhere in the southwestern part of the state we decide to chew up some highway after a snack of sharp white cheddar, sausage, sour dough bread and orange juice.

Road Fish

Despite the beauty of the day and the landscape, subdivided as it is, shadowy, chill intimations disturbing in nature dance among the steep, bouldered and timbered valleys to the east. I feel uneasy. Danger on the rocks is surely here, somewhere. This quest that seems to be morphing into a seriously perverse Bass Masters meat hunt (possibly a slight example here of verbal overkill – on second thought, not really) in my capricious little mind. What the hell. I'm easily lead astray and often proud of it, so play on.

After marveling at the rock walls and cliffs studded with myriad geologic formations that towered over the emerald Wind River below Thermopolis, we spend a full-moon night along the sandstone crested shore of a west-central Wyoming reservoir, At sunrise we hit the road early and manage to kill a week or two waiting for coffee at a kiosk staffed by individuals more interested in making their own specialty concoctions than waiting on paying customers. Then the road climbs up over the southern end of the Wind Rivers glowing in autumn aspen saffron, before drifting lazily past the tourista mining and Oregon Trail townsites of Atlantic City and South Pass City. The day is high altitude, clear blue, late September. Antelope by the hundreds graze, laze and stand casually in the sage flats. We roam the high desert making our way to the town of Kemmerer, home of the original J.C. Penney's store. Gas is cheap here and the residents are friendly. We load up on food and fuel and head out west-northwest towards a river drainage of isolated and obscure dimensions. Turning up a narrow paved road that turns quickly to gravel and dirt we see the tributary we are looking for – a perfectly clear sapphire stream twisting like a sensual snake through golden yellow and orange stands of aspen, willow and alder. Angus and Hereford stand dumbly beneath the still warm sun. Eagles glide.

Hawks circle above soon-to-be-dead rabbits. Mule deer hold on steep sage-pocked slopes. Rounded mountains topped with new snow bend off into the distance. This is paradise in our eyes.

We drop down a steep rocky two-track to the stream, set up camp and head to the water. Beautiful water it is – riffles, runs, pools, undercut banks but after hours of casting all there is to show are a missed one-foot Bonneville and the vanishing site of three tiny trout fleeing for their lives at our approach. We walk back to camp somewhat perplexed but not discouraged. Tomorrow will see us through. A grilled rib-eye and baked potato dinner eaten as the full-moon rises over a steep ridge reinforces our optimism and resolve. Strong black coffee laced with sugar and thick cream drunk within a sparkling sunrise frosty morning furthers our determination.

Along the road a piece, sliding through a steep cutbank of rock, sage and small cactus we work out way upstream for perhaps a half-mile with no luck. Hare's ear nymphs, Elk hair caddis, Royal Wulffs, BWOs – all to no avail. I'd noticed grasshoppers clacking and crash landing in the roadside grasses yesterday and begin to hear them as the day grows warmer. Tying on the rattiest one I have, then greasing the sucker down to make sure it rides high and dry. I launch it to the head of a long, wide, deep aquamarine pool. The bug lands with a "plop." I can smell the slightly creosote scent of the sage as it heats up. A warm breeze slides downstream. A few clouds ride the wind. Magpies and crows argue over something rotten on a nearby rise. The water burbles over and around the cobbled streambed that flashes bright earthy shades of red, tan, ochre, grey and green. The fly drifts slowly to me when I spot an open mouth, white inside of jaws clearly visible as a Bonneville rises slowly from

Road Fish

the river's bottom following the hopper in near-vertical position for five, six feet before taking the bait.

 I set the hook and the trout runs and leaps for twenty feet, then sounds and runs some more before breaking the surface in a spray of crystal to jump for the light several more times. The fish comes to me struggling at this indignity and assault on its natural freedom. I hold the trout and wonder at its design, its colors and its similarity to Yellowstone cutts. Ginny takes a bunch of photos and then the fish is turned loose, disappearing in the green-blue depths. Two more casts produce two more cutthroat like the first one and the day is made and we're happy and back at the Suburban drinking pop, eating sausage and cheese and riding a fine day, one of the finest growing better by the moment.

 As with all road trips, out of the ordinary is par for the course. On the walk back to our rig three stoned, blasted Bozos stop and ask us where to gain access to the water. They're in a painting company truck from Jackson. The clown in the back obviously lost track of his name weeks ago and he contented himself with working on a can of Schlitz (Schlitz?) beer. They tell us they've caught a hundred Bonnevilles and plenty of Czechoslovakian browns with blue stripes above their eyes. The driver tells us they were planted over two-hundred years ago. We eye each other, chat a bit and they vanish in a cloud of dust. I do not see any fishing gear in the cab or the truck's bed. Never heard of blue-streaked eastern European browns and if their planting data is correct the *salmo trutta* described here were dropped in this little stream around the time when Lewis and Clark wandered westward.

 Ah, yes. The joys of conversing with the terminally wasted. I fully understand the concept. We look at each other again and laugh while a turkey vulture offers a widespread wing display on a weathered fence post. The behavior is known as a horaltic pose whose purpose is two bake-off parasites, dry feathers and warm the body. A companion looks on with obvious boredom. These creatures defecate on their own legs, using the evaporation of the water in the feces and/or urine to cool themselves down. There's a fancy scientific name for this, but considering the ostentatious nature of the behavior using the word might be too much. The vultures also projectile vomit on perceived enemies. Wonderful creatures, every one of them.

We finish our lunch and make plans to head for the upper Green River to seek Colorado cutthroat tomorrow morning.

The drive up to an open, grassy flat on the Green River a few miles below Green River Lakes in the Bridger Wilderness is pleasant, scenic and uneventful. We set up camp and decide to enjoy the snow-crested peaks of the Wind River range while cooking dinner. There'd be plenty of time to catch Colorado cutthroats tomorrow and the next day or so I thought. Flat Top Mountain dominated the skyline as it passed through grey-indigo, lemon, orange and then darkening lavender color phases as the sun dropped from the sky.

The next day we fish the river for a couple of miles catching plenty of 8-12 inch wild rainbows. Beautiful fish but not the species we are after. For some reason I'm growing anxious about this and not really enjoying myself like I always do when fishing. Most curious. We decide to hike into the wilderness along the western shore of the lower of the lakes. The wind is severe from the south whipping whitecaps and blowing leaves from the aspens in a steady stream as we work our way several miles to Clear Creek. The stream pours over a natural barricade of granite plummeting 89 feet to

Road Fish

form a shallow pool and then raced downhill through a rocky streambed to join the Green. Flakes of iron pyrite (fool's gold) sparkle among the dark shoreline sands.

Royal and Green Humpies turned numerous small rainbows colored intensely in purple, crimson, dark green and silver with black spotting and bluish parr marks along the flanks, but again no Colorados.

"I thought for sure they'd be in this stream if anywhere," I say to Ginny. "I don't get it. This is crazy."

"Look at the light playing off the waterfall," Ginny says. "Isn't it beautiful? What a great day."

"Yeah. Right," I say all the while wondering where I'll find a Colorado cutt so I can complete this portion of the Slam. I realize that this pursuit is taking over me and spoiling the joy of fishing and Ginny's good time, but those are minor considerations at this point. There is a goal here that needs to be met. I'm obsessed. Driven. Fame and silliness are riding on each cast. The tension is growing, becoming thick, palpable. Can I do this? The imagined crowd looks on in studied silence.

We fish for a couple of hours taking lots of feisty rainbows but no Colorados. We head back to camp, an enjoyable exercise in the late afternoon sun warming us, the dense pine forest across the lake and highlighting mountains that ripped skyward all over the place.

We decide to drive back down south to Big Piney and work the South Piney Creek and its tributary, the Landers Fork. Sage flats and bluffs dotted with oilrigs and storage facilities dominated the landscape as we head into the Wyoming Range. I'm growing restless not catching the Colorado trout and even a bit grumpy. I realize that I've succumbed to a variation of competition fishing and don't like the sensation. Competitive fly fishing – one-fly contest lunacy rising in my head. Enough. Enjoy the rainbows from yesterday, the country I'm passing through the fishing that awaits. At the Landers Fork I rigged up a unique five-foot, two-weight rod – ideal for small, brushy streams like this one. Lots of decent casts to pools and pockets. No fish of any stripe. The same holds true lower down on the South Piney in larger water that is as pretty as any I've seen. Fishless all the same.

One last shot will be along Highway 189 as we head north towards Jackson. At the bridge that spans Cottonwood Creek I get out of the Suburban and peer into the weedy creek. There are a dozen or more Colorado cutthroat. I only want one so I rush back to grab my rod when Ginny points out a large silver Dodge Ram Parked on a ridge above us. Driver's-side window rolled down. I can clearly see a henchmen – no doubt a common laborer for the nearby and as I now notice posted trophy ranch – monitoring us with a pair of large binoculars. Confrontation, harsh words, fisticuffs, gunfire loom on the ugly horizon.

"The hell with it," I say to Ginny. And for some reason the mad compulsion to accomplish the Cutt-Slam goes away. Just like that. Gone. I feel like a sick load of tension has risen from my shoulders and blown away on a western wind. I smile at Ginny and she sees the change and grins back. Life is better now.

We pull back onto 189 and head north. I politely wave at the gentle soul in the Dodge as we pass. No Colorado cutthroat trout. No Cutt-Slam certificate this year, but there's still the legendary fine-spotted Snake River subspecies to chase. Soon we're in the headwaters of the Hoback River and not long after we're up a gravel road and camped alongside a fair-sized tributary. Night is setting in so we make dinner, enjoy a fire and hot tea before turning in.

The morning breaks sunny and clear. The stream

Road Fish

rushes and burbles past our campsite. Steam rises from the water seeming to fluoresce in the light. After coffee I rig up and begin casting a Royal Wulff to all likely holding locations. At a large pool that runs tight to a house-sized boulder a fish rises swiftly to the fly, sets itself, leaps and thrashes before coming to shore. A small Snake River cutt covered in hundreds of tiny jet black spots. Ginny photographs the trout for posterity and this story. I release the fish and it vanishes like it never was here in the first place. A little more fishing a few more trout.

    A fine morning, a great trip that was nearly ruined by my juvenile need to complete the slam of slams. As we drive through eastern Idaho on the way home to Livingston running just west of the backside of the Tetons through aspen groves and pine forest I look back on all of the fish I've caught on the trip – Yellowstone, Bonneville and Snake River cutthroat and those beautiful rainbows, and at the object lesson dealing with the idiocy of anything competitive and fly fishing, hell, any fishing.

    The miles roll by as we wind down the Gallatin Valley. The day is gorgeous, light, color and landscape dancing together in perfect harmony. My thoughts run from how the Cubs are doing to how our black cat Elmer is doing to … Oh Boy! … how I'm going to call a Wyoming fisheries biologist next year about where would be prime Colorado cutthroat water. Where may I expect to take this elusive sub-species? I need that full-color certificate hanging on the bathroom room wall.

    What can be said other than a fool and his desires are a tragic combination.

CHAPTER TWENTY-FOUR
out to lunch

Every man's life ends the same way. It is only the details of how he lived and how he died that distinguish one man from another.
- Ernest Hemingway

"What's that awful sound, John?"
"Out To Lunch by Eric Dolphy."
"Very strange. Is the whole CD like this? Where's the melody?"

"IT'S IN THERE SOMEWHERE and yes it is." I smiled at my companion who looked at me and decided to let the matter drop. Sixties alto sax. Discordant harmonies. Inverted rhythmic phrases. Admittedly Dolphy lacks the stylistic sophistication of the prodigiously talented Kenny G, but then our fishing trips never come close to reaching the rarefied levels of nuance and sophistication as do those delicate, foreign-wines-for-lunch, pampered float trips offered in the glitz ads that are scattered throughout the major fly fishing magazines like dead carp along a muddy bank – the excursions where you absolutely must wear fourteen-thousand bucks of clothing draped with zirconium-encrusted hemostats, stomach pumps, thermometers, and don ball caps plastered with catchy phrases like "I fish, therefore I am."

Perhaps that's an unfair, even harsh line of thought, especially as we slide out of Augusta up a dusty road towards a place we like to fish and camp at along the Sun River. After all, we aren't running down esoteric central Montana trout water in my old beater

Road Fish

pickup anymore, either. We sold out a couple of years back and bought a 1983 GMC Suburban with a roomy back end and a decent sound system. The Suburban is now our only tangible asset, unless you figure in two-hundred fly rods, camera gear, a .357 magnum and a bunch of jazz CDs. At least the rig's windshield is cracked and chipped, the body has a dent or two and the interior reeks of damp waders and soggy crackers creating an ambiance approaching that of the Ft. Peck Inn, a lofty vision in itself. None of this really matters, which is why I'm writing about it. The idea of the whole unplanned, undisciplined journey, the shaky premise we use to justify our inability to hold regular jobs or our very real need to get away from daily interactions with people, is that we live for good country and whatever is found there. And that by photographing and writing about our experiences with intensity and insight we can share the free-form energy and arcane experiences we encounter with others. And we can earn lots of money.

Just another line of bullshit we run by ourselves and scores of unwitting victims from Forsyth to the Port of Del Bonita in a vague attempt to legitimize the insanely good times we have out here in the middle of everywhere doing whatever zips into our heads.

Standing in the wetness of the cool Sun tossing a shredded hopper pattern out into the center of the river with a rhythm turned catatonic through a deleterious combination of heat and repetitious casting is scintillating. To be sure, the casting is at once brilliant and artful with the line unfurling from its tight loop with unerring accuracy fifteen, twenty feet distant, but this is still repetitious, when out of the clear blue water comes a large chunk of determined silver, toothy mouth wide open. The fly is gone and the line on the reel is going, too. A rainbow leaps fifty feet from us, very large, and then falls back to the river and steals more line. The trout leaps again, as far above the water's surface as I've ever seen a freshwater fish go. And this time when the rainbow comes down, it does not drop down into the current, but, instead, flexes its tail flat on the top of the river and thrashes through a hot breeze fast away from me. Lifting gradually backwards on the rod to take up the slack I hear a sound that is a combination of crumpling Saran wrap and breaking stick matches. Something isn't right. I've lost control of the situation. A new experience. Nothing I do with the rod helps and then I look at the pricey piece of graphite. Broken. Shattered just above the handle. Four-hundred bucks of junk and the trout throws the hook with bored disdain. The very large rainbow gleefully arcs through the light, jumping over and over as it heads down river. Pretty to watch. Tough to take, even at this advanced, broken-down stage in the life-long proceedings.

"Nice job, John," she says.

"Not my fault. The damn rod blew up. Cheap piece of crap. Damn good fish down the tubes."

"That's what you always say."

"What do you mean 'always?'"

"That makes five you've wrecked so far and it's not even August. Thank God for Uncle Orvis."

"Thank God, nothing. I think I've been disinherited."

"What'd you do this time, honey?"

"I quit drinking and they don't like the way I dress," and I lit a cigar to ease the pain.

"What's wrong with the way you dress?"

There is nothing like the support and compassion of a good woman to steer you through tough times. I begin to trudge back to camp to grab another rod, her laughter rings in my always-ringing ears. I start to

Road Fish

laugh. Hell, the things have a lifetime guarantee and there are at least fourteen more in the back of the car. Break one. String up another. Onward and upward.

Speaking of which, I look upriver and pray that the ancient, leaking cement structure lyrically known as Gibson Dam, a decrepit edifice that blocks the Sun a couple of miles away hangs on for at least another few days. The idea of being washed away by billions of gallons of unleashed reservoir water, the two of us entwined in a confused jumble of sleeping bags and impaled by tent stakes, all this as we plummet one-hundred-and-fifty feet over the diversion dam roaring a quarter-mile just below us, the image holds little wonder or excitement for me. A couple of divorces, several addictions, numerous intriguing conversations with law enforcement officials and an awfully clear awareness that big money from writing is not in my future are all the thrills I want for this ride. Then again...if I were killed in such a dramatic mishap...maybe my books would sell.

Mid-morning a few days later and the Rocky Mountain Front screams at us from fifty miles away. The outraged mountains dominate our vision with a barrage of intense purple, white, salmon, slate grey and forest green. The small stream we are now fishing flows through a deep cut in the high plains not far below the Alberta border on wide-open tribal land. A friend of ours has given us access to this seldom-fished stretch of water, a couple of miles of lunatic perfection we reach first by highway outside of Browning, a road that diminishes to two-track then finally gives up all pretension of purpose and turns into a chaotic ride across a plowed field of rock and boulders. We park on a cut bank above the water, work our way downstream and start casting the hoppers, always the hoppers for us this time of year.

John Holt

Rainbow trout race to the surface every time the flies hit the water. As soon as the terrestrial imitations land near a midstream obstruction or along an undercut rocky shelf or above a splashing riffle, the fish tag the bugs. All of them are leapers and all of them are healthy fish. Strong, silvery trout that haven't been bothered in years as our friend laughingly assured us earlier in the day. He finds us amusing and is amazed as he says that we "are allowed loose without adult supervision." Knowing how to go invisible helps, helps a lot.

A flat-out amazing stream dancing through arid, empty land. The only sign of humans is an old wooden house, windows broken out, roof long blown away, sideboards weathered a wind-battered grey. If there was a road that led to a bridge that crossed this stream, which there isn't, and if you looked down into the pure water, you'd say "Too shallow and trout don't swim in this kind of country anyway." But the stream is deeper than it looks. Swift runs over bright gravels look skinny when standing on a grassy bank thirty above. Once in the stream, the flow pushes against our stomachs with chilly friendliness as we work upstream. Blue-green pools are ten-feet deep or more, the streambed hidden in darkness.

Four hours of easy fishing makes us believe we have a grip on what we're doing, but we know better. Relatively unfished, unspoiled, damn good water always makes us feel this way. Put us on a pretentious spring creek and we start crying within thirty minutes. Fifteen-foot, 6x leaders. Size 22 patterns. Skillful presentations. Entomological insights. Educated salmonids. Forget it. Size 6 hoppers and 4x tippet are our speed, especially when coupled with wild, cooperative trout.

Much later in the season we stop in at the

Road Fish

Cleveland Bar, an aging wooden joint hiding out in the Bears Paw Mountains. It's Sunday morning. Earlier we fished brush-choked Peoples Creek with tiny dries for little brook trout. Now we are on our way back to the Sun for one last splash before winter shows up. My friend walks into the old, vine-covered place for a quick drink. I stand outside in the breeze, smoking and looking at mountains that appear gentle at first touch, but the more I look the tougher they become. Good country. We could disappear without effort back in here. Raucous laughter ricochets through the screen door and open windows.

"I thought for sure you were from New Hampshire. Live free or die!" roars a deep voice.

"You don't know shit, Tim," this time a feminine one. "Anyone can tell she's from Minnesota. It's in her eyes. Look at them."

I smoke my way through this conversation, riding the wind up a brushy draw, through a grove of aspen and on up to a rocky ridge. Time disappears until my companion exits laughing and shouting over her shoulder "It's in my eyes."

With an inept sense of the appropriate I put on "Low Life" by Donald Bird and we wander off towards the Sun and our campsite several hours away to the west. This time we listen to the music all the way through and I began to think there was at least a small ray of hope for us. And later after pasta with invisible sauce, and grilled vegetables, we sit around the fire watching stars come out and out and out. But we eventually get cold feet and go to sleep.

The wind is insane by the time we crawl out for coffee. Snow, sleet, rain, hail – all of it is coming down, but out of some desperate need to prove to myself and to her that I still am the crazy, take-it-as-it-comes angler of the past, I string the line through the guides and tie on a fat, brown Woolly Bugger. Even ox tippet is elusive in the cold. I settle for a poorly tied clinch knot. The whole thing probably takes twenty minutes and I look around. She's gone. Where now? I wonder. Looking towards the river for the hell of it and there she is standing in the water up to her hips casting into the teeth of a harsh wind. I can see her laughing and can imagine the sound ringing once again in my ears. Way ahead of me as usual.

The hell with "Out To Lunch."

It's high time for Ornette Coleman's "Snowflakes And Sunshine."

Thank you for reading.
Please review this book. Reviews help others find Absolutely Amazing eBooks and inspire us to keep providing these marvelous tales.

If you would like to be put on our email list to receive updates on new releases, contests, and promotions, please go to AbsolutelyAmazingEbooks.com and sign up.

About the Author

John Holt is the author of over two dozen published books including *Hunted in Paradise, Plain Crazy in Paradise, Blown Away Under the Big Sky, The Lost Patrol, Yellowstone Drift – Floating the Past in Real Time, Arctic Aurora – Canada's Yukon and Northwest Territories, Coyote Nowhere – In Search of America's Last Frontier*. His work has appeared in such publications as *Men's Journal, Fly Fisherman, High Country News, Crossroads, E – The Environmental Magazine, Big Sky Journal, The Fly-fish Journal* and *Gray's Sporting Journa*l. He and his wife, photographer Ginny, live in Livingston, Montana.

The New Atlantian Library

AbsolutelyAmazingEbooks.com
or AA-eBooks.com

www.ingramcontent.com/pod-product-compliance
Lightning Source LLC
Chambersburg PA
CBHW070534170426
43200CB00011B/2426